MW00583695

Dear Don,

Here is the "Green Alpha".

IDEAS FOR AMERICA

Let the Sun In

Matthew J. Fraser

Matthew J. Fraser 8/18/15

Salem, MA

Salem House Press

PO Box 249

Salem MA 01970

ISBN- 10: 0-9836665-3-9

ISBN- 978-0-9836665-3-0

First Edition 2012

This Land Was Made for You and Me

All children should experience the wonders of our national parks. Expansion of our park system would be great for the soul of the nation and perhaps help us work together on other, more complicated issues.

| Preface |

If you want to get right to the ideas and themes for discussion, then you can skip this section. However, if you wanted to know more about the journey of writing this book, then you might want to read the introduction, which is the product of a nineteen year journey. In short, *Ideas for America; Let the Sun In* integrates some of the best research and ideas together into a book designed to be a useful tool in our time of need.

European Influences

The two and a half years I spent in Europe from 1995-1997 were absolutely essential to my development as a student and language teacher. Missing a Swedish girl in 1994, in early 1995 I began studying Swedish as much as five hours day. I left my real estate job in Boston to go work as an au-pair for a wealthy German family in Frankfurt, Germany. That job was my first experience taking care of children and led to my eventually getting my start teaching languages in Bonn, Germany. I studied the German and Russian language many hours a day, taught at language schools and was profoundly influenced by some of the very high quality public facilities, in particular the local sports clubs, walking and bike options and municipal recreational facilities. These experiences helped to shape both my educational philosophies and perspective on what a healthy community really is.

The Return to the States

In October of 1997 I left a beautiful family in Europe to come home because I knew if I stayed in my wonderful life I would eventually have to watch America struggle as I watched powerlessly from the other side of the ocean. So, I left my little paradise to come home and begin reading, learning and writing. The only phrase I remember writing overseas was in the library in Siegburg, Germany, which was; "the two political parties battling it out will not solve our problems." Little did I know then how polarized we would later become! One strong memory from my stay in Europe was the quality and fun had at the municipal pools; since then I have dreamed of having such facilities in New England.

The Early Years

When I first sat down to write I had no idea what to say; I only knew I needed to find ideas and principles that readers could learn from and apply. In 1998 and 1999 I worked as a building superintendent in Brighton, Mass., the routine of washing floors, vacuuming and taking out the garbage provided nice breaks in between reading and writing. After reading a few reports on health care and education at the Boston College Library, I found the gem upon which all other research could be built; "The State of the

American Dream," put out by the "evidence-based" Massachusetts research group *MassInc.* Their insights on education (in particular vocational education) helped to form the core upon which other research and ideas could be built.

Commitment to Teaching and Labor

One aspect of the journey was my commitment to not taking any jobs that interfered with writing. This meant I took only labor work (which relaxed for the evening's writing and research) or teaching jobs, as the latter kept me connected with the needs and struggles of young people. Whereas teaching English from 1995 to late 1997 in Germany at language schools, would later yield insights into language education in the U.S., working as a high school Spanish teacher from 2000 until 2005 would give me valuable experience to learn from. From 2000-2001 I taught at Newman Prep in Boston, although during the four years after that headed north to teach at a school in a New Hampshire resort community.

The Waterville Valley Years

Through the years of writing the book, one aspect that I had not anticipated took on a life of its own; the heartache and stress from fifteen years of isolation. Most of those I had gone to school with were now investment bankers, salesmen or other well-paid professionals. By contrast, I was making an average of about $15,000 a year doing landscaping, "high risk" special education or other unglamorous work. In short, people stop calling and eventually even answering my calls. For one period I had to live in an unheated attic in Brookline, just a stone's throw from the beautiful house where I grew up. The truth is that it got to me, although struggling alone taught me the value of many creative approaches to building physical and mental health, not to mention the ideas on building healthy local economies.

However, the years 2001-2005 were significant because I had the time to continue to develop ideas on education and quality of life. Living and teaching in Waterville Valley with free faculty housing gave me time to develop some book principles. I took care of a nice dog and some nights I would take her to a platform on the other side of a cemetery on Boulder Way to practicing asking and answering questions related to the book. The platform was beneath a beautiful, starry sky and overlooked a river in a canyon below. Almost every night I practiced asking and answering the question "how do we maximize education to help young people."? Over time I came to answer this core question in a more complete way, which is reflected in the ten highly developed chapters of the book. At the end of the day though, the real question I'm trying to answer is the same; "what do people need to be happy and healthy and how do we assure that they get it"?

The Birth of New Hope Rises

Over the years notes became paragraphs and paragraphs pages. Pages became chapters and on August 8th, 2005, the rough ancestor of this work was published, *Ideas for America; New Hope Rises.* It was a really good start, a work of core principles to be built on. However, our ever-changing world and news crises spurred me to continue to write. Responses to the mortgage crisis of 2007, ideas on health care, free expression, world peace and reducing cruelty to animals were integrated into later updates. By 2008 cracks in the well-being of our country were beginning to show themselves (the mortgage crisis) and I did my best to respond with relevant updates in 2009 and 2011.

Special Education Years: 2007-2009

In 2007-2008 I took a job in northeastern Massachusetts working with young people with severe emotional and neurological disorders, students who were too unwell to be in school. Each day I spent two hours with a grammar school student, two hours with a middle school student and two hours with a high school student. The idea was just to continue the curriculum, and I found myself teaching all sorts of subjects I never thought I would. It was sad to see these young people struggling so much, especially considering how hard they were trying. This experience further influenced my interest in and emphasis on fundamentals such as healthy school lunches, walking and biking paths, teaching personal finance and quality physical education in creating .

In the first seven months of 2009 I worked as a Title 1 tutor, during which time I had many assignments, including working as a Russian translator, doing Kindergarten inclusion, first grade guided reading, 6th grade English and 6th grade Math, sometimes in Spanish. However, although I did gain some knowledge through this work, it was not until I took an Adolescent Psychology course at Salem State (necessary for teacher certification) in 2013 that I was able to make sense of all the varied teaching experiences. It was Professor LaCroix with his over forty years of experience that brought alive themes in "family mapping" and special education in a way that would help me to think more constructively about ways to help children and adolescents.

Going Zen and Green

An unexpected boost came from studying Jiu-jitsu and Thai kickboxing at *Dragon Within Martial Arts;* the workouts would give me the balance and well-being to feel good most of the time. Even better that I've still only scratched the surface of the two arts; it's good to know that in the years to come I will have a system for building my health and well-being, not to mention having a lot of fun. Having the mind set that I do, of course I think about the positive effect these two activities could have on young people.

In 2009 I began to work as a language tutor, helping students perform better in school and adults acquire a skill. In December of 2010 an old friend told me to watch the PBS special "Fixing the Future," a program which gave me the new ideas to transform the work into a more powerful problem-solving resource with a new focus; local economies. It was the second work by PBS that yielded powerful ideas, the first being a special on preventing dog euthanasia.

The Green Years

The predecessor of this book had a section on the environment and expansion of the national park system, but there was not much on green energy. However, reading *Winning Our Energy Independence* by David Freeman helped to expand the scope of ideas related to renewable energy and local farming. In August of 2012 *Ideas for America; Let the Sun In* was published.

From August of 2012 until March of 2015, I continued to work a little on the book every day by integrating the themes of the different chapters. Those years were tough as I watched our country struggle and hit all kinds of new lows, including what I see as extreme conformity, a serious hostility to new ideas. I then recognized the need not just for a book of ideas, but for a whole new generation of authors, journalists, citizens and college classes to respond to our challenges. So, my emphasis became to produce a handbook for them. That said, good luck to you I wish you well finding what it is that you can do for your community.

Matthew J. Fraser

Contents

The Importance of the Conversation

The way in which the many ideas in this book are analyzed is more important than the ideas themselves. First, there are many themes here that can be explored by new authors as a full book. Second, local newspapers can do the next generation a real service by focusing on how they can benefit students in the towns they cover. Third, although many universities are already exploring themes in education, interfacing with both school and local papers could add a whole new dimension to conversations on making education really work.

1

Education

Well, if you want to sing out, sing out

And if you want to be free, be free

'Cause there's a million things to be

You know that there are

- *Cat Stevens, Harold and Maude*

In this chapter we'll be looking at specifically how we can utilize education to help the younger generation build a bright future. We will look at perspectives of top researchers on special education and how they can create great the opportunities for happy days at school. Particular attention is also given to ways to maximize language programs at both the K-12 and university levels. A language teacher by profession, I utilize my experiences to analyze existing, successful approaches to learning at both levels.

The ideas here on education are at the core of much of this book. When I began taking notes and researching, I didn't believe that it would be so. However, over time I've come to see just how much effective schools and dynamic universities can contribute to quality of life. This chapter only touches on the subject. Also particular attention is given to ways to maximize language programs at both the K-12 and university levels. A language teacher by profession, I utilize my experiences to analyze existing, successful approaches to learning at both levels.

But, my Main Goal is to present all these ideas in a way that students and parents, new authors, teachers and journalists can expand upon the ideas here. The themes in this chapter could easily be expanded into fifty books by ambitious authors.

Chapter One Concerns

A. NEW EDUCATION STANDARD- Share core principles about the role of vocational education, teaching personal finance, testing, quality physical education, special education, private schools, model language programs and adult education.

B. WHAT IS WORKING ALREADY-Look at existing, successful walk-to-school models and efforts to provide healthier school lunches. The goal is to integrate analysis of these two fundamental aspects of wellness into discussions on education and the health of children.

...

Why is the Cat Stevens song quote at the beginning of the chapter? That quote expresses the core belief that people need to be themselves, to let out all the magic inside them. In education that students need to work on being the best version of who they are, which can allow us just to enjoy life.

...

NEW EDUCATION STANDARD

Vocation Schools

One under utilized opportunity to give students the tools they need to survive and thrive is greater use of vocational programs. Currently in Massachusetts, only seven percent of students attend vocational schools, although the research of MassInc. has led me to believe that thirty to forty percent of students would be better off in vocational programs. (1) The first issue with the present situation is that too many of the thirty to forty percent of students who should be in a vocational program graduate from high school with a second rate traditional education, not to mention few marketable skills. In many cases they are not going on to college, and their devalued high school diploma doesn't open the doors that it once did.

The trend in recent years has been of America splitting into two halves; the haves and the have-nots, and it's important to ensure that our focus in education is to combat this dichotomy. We should focus on emphasizing vocational education to give young people the skills they need to thrive in our global economy. Combine this kind of skill acquisition with teaching the basics of mortgage and finance and we can give more students the tools they need to survive and thrive.

What are the effects of under utilization of vocational programs? As a teacher I can say that both teaching and learning are difficult in a class of thirty when ten to twelve students shouldn't or don't want to be there. Why not let more students discover if carpentry or electrical work is for them? I am not in favor of European style exams that determines a student's placement, but the choice of high school program should not simply be a matter of conformity. Another aspect to consider is the fact that we in America need to rebuild our manufacturing base, but to do that we are going to need workers with skills. In short, we need to create the workforce with the skills to rebuild our economy.

Are there any unique perspectives on the utilization of vocational education? Yes. In their report *The State of the American Dream*, the group *MassInc.* stated that not only would thirty to forty percent of students be better off in a vocational high school, but as many as half would be better off with a combination of traditional and vocational programming. (2) This dynamic, flexible approach might be just what the generation growing up in this economy needs. Many aren't up to a complete shift to vocational schooling, but our economy desperately needs to close the skills gap.

What are the causes of the under utilization of vocational education? In my experience teaching there are two main reasons for the current imbalance between vocational and traditional schooling. The first reason is parental pressure; the simple fact that many parents insist that their child go to a vocational school. However, I believe that since the last time I taught high school in 2005, the attitudes have changed. In this economy parents just want something that can get their kid a job.

The second cause of this imbalance may be the influence of educational "purists" who believe that all learning should be book learning. In my opinion our culture puts pressure on children to go to college and to follow the traditional path, which is easy to understand considering the devaluation of a high school diploma. As the cost of living increases this parental perspective is understandable, but we need to adjust and realize just how much young people can benefit from a practical education and marketable skills.

A third force preventing restoration of more vocational education may be those who don't believe one should receive a high school diploma for vocational studies. They look down upon anything other than book education. However, in the current economy this attitude has grown scarce.

A fourth reason for this imbalance maybe that many vocational educators are happy with their current status of relative independence from state control. It should not be forgotten that the purpose of education is to prepare students for the world, not just to flatter an educator's idea of what education should be. It is far better for students to have a decent knowledge of reading and mathematics, combined with an applicable, vocational skill than to be driven to despair in the current job market. A student with basic reading and math skills, a trade and knowledge of personal finance can effectively make his or her way in the world.

Personal Finance

I emphasize the importance of understanding the basics of personal finance and credit from both my own experience and listening to students talk about their future, and hearing the lack of certainty and understanding. I myself was twenty-eight years old before I had this knowledge and it was not until I had this knowledge that saving money or increasing income meant much to me. I believe that the same goes for most other young people; they need to acquire this knowledge somehow to make their way in the world.

Why is this knowledge necessary? It is very hard for a student to clearly envision what is monetarily possible without understanding the basics of mortgages, budgeting, renting and credit. If a young person is working or trying to choose a trade, it is important to know not only how much money he will earn in that trade, but also what is possible to do with that money. If a student knows that by becoming a carpenter he might earn $40,000 a year, and also understands how mortgages work, he can imagine what sort of house and lifestyle he might afford on that wage. He or she also might begin planning better at an earlier age, as opposed to being overwhelmed by it all.

Do you know any success stories? Whenever I talk about vocational education, I think of the story of the nephew of an acquaintance—Will. Like many students, Will had never been very interested in traditional school, and saw it as something that he just had to do. He found his course work to be boring and irrelevant to his life. His sophomore year he made the switch to a regional technical school and flourished there. As someone highly intelligent who simply prefers experiential learning, he had the stimulation he needed to be very successful. He was able to get a basic traditional education while learning a trade. At 19, he was working under a master electrician part time while completing his course work. According to his aunt, his self-esteem has increased incredibly. As a result of the vocational training and learning the basics of mortgages and credit, Will enjoys life and can build a stable financial future.

What is the best way to teach personal finance in the schools? There are many ways to communicate this knowledge this to young people, including auditorium presentations, classroom presentations and as part of the curriculum. Auditorium presentations are by the most affordable; although I believe that integrating the study of mortgages, financing, renting and credit into math class is the best approach.

Testing

My goal with this section is not to advocate for or against testing, but rather to give multiple perspectives that parents and students might use.

The Angry Mother Bear. I had one experience in 2004 that strongly influenced my opinions on testing. While running for state office on an education platform, I was asked by a mother with a learning disabled daughter if I was in favor of the MCAS, a Massachusetts test that students must pass to graduate. I said yes, I was in favor of the tests; at that time my understanding was that they were a good tool for raising standards, which is especially important for students coming from low-income backgrounds, ones for whom education is a way up. The mother then looked me dead in the eyes and yelled at me, telling me how cruel it was for her learning disabled daughter to not receive a diploma after having gone to high school every day and trying her best, only to be denied a diploma because she just wasn't up to passing the test. The truth of the matter is that at that time I had no answer and just had to listen as the angry mother bear vented her frustrations.

Over years of teaching experience I developed a more effective answer to the angry mother bear. At the time I had emphasized the original four points in this book; more vocational education, teaching personal finance, more effective physical programs and interactive language programs. I still do believe that each of these four points can have a positive effect on *everyone*, but they still are not a complete answer to the mother's tears of frustration. However, after ten more years of teaching, educational coursework and life, I see more clearly that *everyone* needs to have a clear path to success, which means we're going to have to be smarter and more flexible in how we help out young people.

Another conclusion is that it would be a shame to restrict ourselves to getting rid of testing in Special Education, to think that this was the sole way to liberate the younger generation. Rather, we need to respond in every way we can; in the section on Special Education in this chapter you'll read about a few of those ways. However, the ideas in Chapter Four on healthy local economies are also relevant; vibrant local economies create opportunities for learning, building relationships and even employment. Additionally, the ideas in Chapter Eight can help to transform the college experience into one where not only test takers can thrive, but also those with a love of life, students who are eager to help make the world the best place it can possibly be.

OK, but what are the main reasons for testing? In order to raise standards there has to be a standard. In order to know what students have learned; for administrators and parents to plan, there has to be some measurement of success. In Massachusetts there are essentially two kinds of tests; minimum standards tests and subject assessment tests. In the next pages we'll reflect on the reasoning behind this system and if and how it serves young people well.

Do you have any reservations about testing students? It pains me to think that students that are trying so hard, only to be put down by a culture that overvalues testing, material success and superficiality. I arrived at this position more strongly after taking a course in Adolescent Psychology (necessary for certification), in which I learned about the system of tracking, whereby students were put in low level courses, which had a tendency for students to work alone with worksheets. Test results could cause this placement, but makes this system tough to take is that poor students are more often put into the lower levels, which must lead to feelings of being a second class citizen or cast aside.

What is another issue to be addressed that relates to testing? After watching the movie *A Place at the Table*, (3) I was alerted to the fact that many children go to school hungry. And, what greater shame is there than subjecting children to judgement when the adults are not feeding them. There are a number of people working hard to solve this problem, which of course is money related. One person working to change things is British Chef Jamie Oliver, who has taken on the challenge of feeding children within a budget, which you can read about at jamieoliver.com

Another reservation comes if students can't concentrate because of something bothering them then they won't be able to perform on a test well. I know this from personal experience; I failed both the teacher's test and a real estate exam, basically because I couldn't relax. By the same token I can only imagine how much pressure it puts on students to have to worry about not receiving a diploma if they can't pass a test to graduate.

What testing do you believe is good for quality education? I think that "minimum standard" and subject assessment tests are necessary in order to ensure that children are learning. Unlike the basic skills test, I don't believe that there should be a minimum score to graduate, but test scores should give students, teachers and administrators an idea of how much has been learned. I came to this opinion independently after two years of teaching and research, but some have arrived at quite different opinions, such as the lunch lady turned union president Lily Eskelsen-García, who believes that we need "put the brakes on stupid education reform and telling politicians to leave teaching to the professionals." (4)

While I don't believe that students be judged as people by test scores, my only bias as a language teacher is my hope to some measure of achievement that will allow children to have fun and acquire a skill in their language classes.

What is the role of minimum standards tests? Minimum standards tests respond to the growing number of people who lack the basic skills of reading, writing and arithmetic. I read a one hundred and five page report titled "New Skills for the New Economy." (5) I wasn't sure what I would learn — perhaps a need for more people with computer or technology skills? What I found was a real need for people who had the basic skills-reading, writing, and arithmetic. The Massachusetts equivalent of the basic skills test, the MCAS, is a scored test, but in function is essentially a pass/fail exam. If you pass you graduate, if you don't you don't. (6)

Naturally it's a problem there are some who don't pass the MCAS test every year, but arguably a greater problem is when the high school diploma doesn't guarantee skills or employment. In theory minimum standards tests can help to assure that a high school diploma has value, and as such are given serious consideration by policy makers.

What is the role of subject assessment tests? Whereas a minimum standard test assures that all graduates have basic skills or knowledge, subject assessment tests assure knowledge in a specific subject area. For many students, passing a minimum standards test is not very challenging, but subject assessment tests let them show off how much they've learned in a particular subject

How do subject assessment tests curb grade inflation? Currently, an A, B, or a C in a specific subject doesn't guarantee as much to a potential employer as it used to. It all depends on the school, the level of the class, and the teacher. The idea behind subject assessment tests can provide the structure to assure that student performance is recognized.

How can subject assessments affect quality of world language programs? If done right, quite a bit. After teaching in language schools with very specific goals and assessment it was hard to make the transition to high school. In high school, my assignment was to get through the book, with no effective measurement of how much facility with the Spanish language students had acquired. This works fine in some subjects, but languages are living entities that require new kinds of assessment, such as a high emphasis on participation.

Testing in Language Classes. I've been a language teacher for eighteen years, including five at the high school level, so I naturally have thoughts about how testing can work for language classes. Having a standard test that shows accomplishment in a language could help to assure that students acquire a skill from five years of studying a language. Ideas might be an emphasis on participation *and* assessment.

Why is participation as important as testing in language class? There is no substitute for students with a great attitude that do the oral drills well and work with students that are struggling to help them do better. For that and other reasons I go into in the section on language learning later in this chapter, I believe making the participation grade count for as much as thirty to forty percent can be a good idea, if students are truly encouraged to let all the magic inside them come out. So, we need both pieces of the puzzle; recognizing students that bring out the best and themselves in others through classroom practice and a test that measures practical oral, written and reading abilities.

Physical Education

The focus here is to look at how physical education programs can be used to maximize quality of life for young people. Ideally, not only will physical education give students the exercise they need to relax in their learning environment, but they also will acquire the skills and knowledge to live healthier lives. As in other sections of this book I find it helpful to use a question and answer format to both make the points here more specific, as well as putting the information in chunks students can digest.

Why are physical education programs so under utilized? After working for seven years in grammar and high schools, including two in special education, I noticed that few of the behavioral problems and attention difficulties students faced were addressed with physical activity. I wondered if maybe the reason was the focus on team sports; a great outlet for some. What I was looking for was a physical program that could provide everyone with the exercise they need to feel their best. What follows are my findings in question and answer form.

What is the relationship between healthy school food and physical education? For students to get the maximum benefits of physical education they need to eat well. This is why the efforts of people like Jamie Oliver, movies like *Les Enfants Nous Accuseront* and others are so important. The more we can analyze, promote and celebrate people like this, the better the chances are that the healthiest possible food will make it to the schools, which in turn will hopefully lead to the well-being to better enjoy physical programs.

Might inclusive physical programs help with bullying? Physical life skills classes such as martial arts, dance, or weight lifting can give students the exercise, skills and well-being they need. It's also important because this kind of inclusion can help prevent bullying. Although there still is plenty of aggressive, direct bullying, the modern version involves complicated psychological attacks, the goals of which is often to isolate the victim. Check out the article in the End Notes from the No Bullying website to learn more.

At the end of the day, the emphasis of this chapter with regards to bullying is the promotion of dynamic, integrated schools, which alone should help to prevent bullying in all of its many forms. I believe we can work together with ideas in this chapter can create schools where students are so communal, dynamic and integrated that bullying has little space to grow.

What is one way to find the time for physical education? One answer is for students to be able to do physical education instead of study hall. Having served as a proctor for many study halls, it pained me to be so strict with students when I knew that some of them just really needed to take a break from academics and get some exercise. It just seemed totally unrealistic and unfair to have to reprimand students who couldn't sit perfectly still with book learning all day – don't they deserve to run around and have some fun once in a while?

Is there any existing research that can shed light on the state of physical education programs? According to the Centers for Disease Control, "Nearly half — 46 percent — of high school students were not attending any P.E. classes when surveyed by the Centers for Disease Control; still others have P.E. for only one-third of the year." (7) I had no trouble believing this statistic after difficult experiences with agitated students in study halls. For parents dealing with how to advocate for more physical education, it would be helpful if local newspapers did some good journalistic work and looked at ways that research on physical education done around the country could be applied to benefit young people. Considering that only nine percent of people get their news from newspapers, (compared with 55% from television and 21% from the Internet) (8) exploring the potential of physical education to contribute to quality of life locally could be a great, new avenue for local papers to explore.

Are there any good examples of university coursework that meets the physical needs of students? Colleges can also serve students well by teaching them physical skills. A course called "Healthy Lifestyle 101," that met five days a week at eight in the morning could give students a healthy start to their day. The seventy-five minutes of kickboxing, dance, cardio or strength building workouts could be combined with a short daily reading on nutrition or physiology. It would be interesting to see what examples there are of this at the college level. (9)

As for the value of good journalism on subjects such as physical education, it should also be noted just how little appreciation good journalism often gets. I was awakened to this fact on an edition of *Beat the Press* on PBS, during which four journalists I respect were lamenting the tendency for journalists to do hard research, only to have the people on television talk about it without any attribution to the source. At first glance you may say "what does this have to do with physical education," but the fact is that if journalists are going to work hard to provide information that can help struggling young people, they need to be rewarded for it.

One of the themes of this book is to promote the value of local newspapers in the modern world, to point out how they can be useful in many situations, including education policy. However, for that to happen the right way, community leaders need to identify their wants and needs and communicate that to their local newspapers. In some cases community members may even want to consider reestablishing local control of their papers, rather than get their news from corporate giants with headquarters thousands of miles away. Perhaps a localization of media would allow communities to explore ideas in physical education and other subjects the way they need to respond to the needs of young people. This are just my thoughts, they are for you to explore!

What is a good report on the value and reasons for physical education? "Top 10 Reasons for Quality Physical Education" by Guy Le Masurier and Charles B. Corbin articulates one core truth well, stating; "Taking time from physical education does not result in more learning in other areas." (10) However, this is just one small quote from the paper; there are many other good points that advocates of a healthier, more active school can utilize in the struggle to assure that children get the exercise they need in school.

Will physical education teachers be the 21st century profession? A second point made by Le Masurier and Corbin quoted historian Roberta Parks, who noted that "During the 20th century, medicine emerged as the renaissance profession because of the development of a sound scientific base." However she argued that physical education teacher "has become the renaissance profession of the new millennium" (11) After all, who is in a greater position to contribute to the well-being of children than the teacher that supervises the daily exercise of young boys and girls?

Are there any good studies on the value of physical education for young girls? How can this be part of the whole picture of physical and mental health for girls? Luckily, yes, because many young girls are struggling for their physical and mental health. Myra and David Sadker wrote; (12)

"Somewhat more confident about their physical abilities and other talents in earlier years, young girls of ages 10 through 13 experience a psychological reversal in their development. Cultural messages and societal pressures substantially affect their development and drive them into a downward psychological tailspin resulting in stifled academic and motoric achievement records. The critical period of time for girls has been identified as early adolescence." (13)

One good response is good, dynamic physical programs, which provides a time when girls can just have fun, not be under the constant pressures that our culture puts on them. That said, this alone isn't going to help the problem; what we need is nothing less than a spiritual revolution.

Special Education

For me, talking about ways for special education students to feel better and progress is exciting, because I now know that there are so many ways that we can do better by them. Looking back on two often challenging years working with students with severe emotional and neurological disorders, I wish I had known more about some initiatives I've learned about while writing this book. I did the best I could, but there are positive changes we can make, ones that can make a big difference to students in the future.

Statistics on the Growth of Special Education. Between 2006 and 2010, the number of Massachusetts students with serious health problems was up 59%, with the number of students with neurological disorders up 35%. (14)

17 percent of Massachusetts students are in special education programs, compared with a national average of 13 percent. The rate in Massachusetts jumps to 23 percent for low-income students, who spend much of their day in separate classrooms. (15)

The Need for a Holistic Approach. To truly help young people in special education we need to make improvements both inside and outside of school. Specifically, we need to look at walk-to-school programs, school lunches, local economy initiatives and physical education to fully meet the needs of young people. Another response is to look at how vocational education might work better for students struggling with traditional studies. Perhaps we might find a win-win response by both helping students acquire skills to help us rebuild our manufacturing base.

Struggling Children; Canaries in the Coal Mine. Children struggling in school can be seen as are the "canaries in the coal mine", because the steps we need to take for them to adjust to the world are the same ones that the world needs. By that I mean that building the healthier, more joyful schools for struggling children will benefit all schoolchildren.

What is the cause of the growth of special education? The report "The Rising Costs of Special Education" stated; "the root causes of these increases have been factors beyond the control of the schools, such as advances in medical technology; the de-institutionalization of children with special needs, privatization of services and economic and social factors including increases in the number of children living in poverty and the number of families experiencing social and economic stress." (16) This quote is important because it shows that the source of the growth is not lax social attitudes, but rather very real environmental and biological factors.

What role can the "local economy" play for children struggling in school? As a Safe Routes video asserts, walking and bike paths can give children opportunities to get exercise and explore their world. (17) A robust local farming system can help provide high quality school food, green space and learning opportunities on the farm. The time banking system can help create symbiotic relationships between young people, although this is an as yet relatively undeveloped system; the only such example I am aware of in New England being the *Coalition for a Better Acre* in Lowell, Massachusetts. (18)

What are some effects of the large size of special education? First, paying for special education often absorbs a great deal of the school budget, which arguably can indirectly lead to larger classroom size and therefore less personalized attention for the average student. (19) In Massachusetts, 50% of the Education budget is spent on the 17% of students in Special Education. (20)

Second, teachers often have to modify teaching style to accommodate these students, such as putting certain students in the first row, which isn't a big deal unless there are ten other students in the class that also need special attention. So, there are plenty of ideas to explore in special education outside the classroom; now let's look at some ideas inside the classroom.

Vocational Education and Special Education. Under utilized vocational education may lead to more students struggling in the traditional classroom setting whereas they might be better off learning hands on, marketable skills. In Massachusetts, only seven percent of students are in vocational programs, although in the opinion of *MassInc.*, thirty to forty percent of students would be better off in vocational studies, while as many as fifty percent should be doing a combination of vocational and traditional studies. (21) "Comprehensive" high schools, or those that have traditional and vocational programs on one campus may have a programming advantage in that doing a combination of traditional and vocational studies is more feasible.

Art and Expressive Programs. Two years in special education working with those with severe emotional and neurological disorders taught me the power of daily art class during all four years of high school. In a school day that can feel long and stressful, there's nothing like one period during which everyone is happy. Students acquired skill sets that compounded during the course of the years in school and by junior and senior year were often doing amazing work. So, how will we find the time and money for this? That's what we need to figure out.

How can universities adapt to students that have traditionally had a hard time with book learning? I don't like thinking about it so much as adapting to students with special needs, but rather focusing on helping empower students that want to contribute to quality of life. We desperately need people that can reintroduce locally grown food to their community, help in the development of walking and bike paths or just change the culture so everyone has a chance to feel great. To that end, Chapter Eight offers thirty ways our universities can promote a healthier, sustainable lifestyle. I believe that when our colleges place a priority on producing creative contributors and healers, the students will come.

What is "tracking" and how is it relevant to Special Education? "Tracking," the practice of putting students in low or high level classes has three main problems. The first is that there is often very little mobility, meaning that students can be stuck there for their whole school career. The second problem is the stigmatization that comes with being in the lower track, which can be tough to deal with emotionally. The third issue is the tendency for struggling students to be taught with strategies "dominated by strategies that are passive; students do lots of worksheets, they tend to work alone." According to recent articles on tracking, students need rich content, group problem-solving activities and interaction with their peers. I believe that a good look at this system, healthy lunches and walk-to-school programs will help a great deal .

What is some good reading on tracking? One good article on tracking was by Anne Wheelock in the October 1992 publication of *Educational Leadership* titled "The Case for Untracking."(22) In that article she discusses "dismantling unproductive grouping practices that have undermined education for all but a few students." She goes on to emphasize a number of key principles, including "A Belief that All Students can Learn and "A Belief in Change as a Process." A second article on tracking is "On Restructuring Schools: A Conversation with Al Shanker; Making the Best of Schools."

As for Al Shanker, his story is an interesting one; he was not only the President of the American Federation of Teachers but is also credited with being the originator of the idea of charter schools, an aspect of education that is not addressed here.

How does current policy affect choice for primary and secondary school teachers? Like students, teachers also need to be happy to be effective. One teacher told me a story of an advanced placement English class, which was his greatest pleasure and much of the reason he continued teaching.

Up until a few years ago, he was able to choose who came into his advanced English class. That all changed as the power of parents continued to grow. If a parent wanted his or her child to be in the class, at least in this school there was little a teacher could do to stop it. In some cases, the students had severe problems with the English language and struggled in lower level classes, but he now lacked the authority and respect to decide what standards were appropriate for those who entered his class. In my view the teacher should have the final say as to who enters the high level courses.

Private Schools

This section has a few perspectives on the role of grammar schools, private schools and adult education. Some of these observations are based on teaching experience, others on conclusions of the sources. As with the other sections of the book, I encourage readers to not limit themselves to my little opinions, but rather to go to the End Notes and Bibliography to read the source articles and make this book the beginning, not the end of a journey.

The Role of the Grammar Schools. Based on experience teaching, research and conversations with grammar school teachers, it's only at the grammar school level that goals should be relatively uniform. Children learn at different speeds, but the goals should be to build basic skills. Only if the grammar schools are successful in their mission do high school programs have a chance to work well for students. However, the goal here is to find two points most of us can agree on; healthy school lunches and walk-to-school programs.

Is hunger an issue at grammar schools as well? Yes. You might think serious childhood hunger is rare in the United States, but according to the movie *A Place at the Table* it's quite common. According to the movie, part of the problem is a pre-conceived notion of what hungry looks like. Some of the children going hungry might have a healthy weight but they're getting very little nutrition, which can mean the children look normal but don't feel good enough to focus at school.

Are there any people or organizations working to find ways to serve children the best food possible? Yes. Two movies that look at the potential of healthy school food are *Les Enfants Nous Accuseront* (French) and *A Place at the Table*. The British Chef Jamie Oliver has also done extensive work on his show

The Role of the Private Schools. I have encountered one major misconception about private schools; they get the best students and therefore naturally succeed. While some of the more elite schools do get some of the best and brightest, many of the students I've known who attended private schools also go there because the public schools did not work for them. I am now speaking strictly from my own teaching experiences, but I've found that the private schools are simply a better fit for some children. Some of this may be related to greater funding, but much may have to do with better organization and the freedom to choose who comes and goes.

Recently, the graduates of private schools have had a more difficult time with their graduates getting into the best colleges. The reason for this may be political as colleges are trying to get away from an old elitist system.

One of the ways that private schools can respond to the increasing difficulty in getting students into colleges is through adoption of some of the ideas on more effective language study outlined in this chapter. Although they cannot control the choices of college admissions, the administration and parents can support more fun, effective language learning with the right support of teachers. This is something they *can control* that will lead to greater student success.

What are some aspects of private school evaluations? I don't know if what independent schools inspectors do in 2015 is different from 2005, but when I was working at private schools from 2000-2005 the aspects they looked at were often physical, such as the number of computers or the size of the library. In the future inspector might look at aspects that relate to student well-being.

What is their role of testing? It can raise standards; we just need to not also break hearts. The school at which a friend teaches has a very good English program; junior year take either the Advanced Placement or SAT II English exam. For the four or six years they're in the school, the curriculum is roughly based on preparing them for the test. Some see this as teaching to the test, but there is also room for a great deal of creativity. With this approach, every time students ask "is it going to be on the test," the teacher can say "yes."

How can private schools lead the way in quality language instruction? One way is to base a good percentage of the grade on participation. A hard working student that tries hard to do the classroom drills well while helping out classmates is a big plus and should be rewarded. Basing as much as 40% of the grade on participation can help foster the kind of environment that will help students acquire real speaking skills. In my professional experience private or charter schools on any budget with students of any ability level can pass on language skills to students while having fun with this approach. Also, private schools tend to be smaller, and some might argue that this small size creates greater cohesion between students.

This book advocates greater use of vocational programs yet private schools emphasize traditional book learning, right? My limited experience speaking with private school administrators and teachers tells me that vocational programs are very much making a comeback. Many use vocational programs to acquire practical skills while enhancing personal growth. Many private schools have very good wood working and arts programs; someone could write a very helpful book focusing just on this.

What are other ways private schools can respond? Some private schools have more resources and choice when it comes to integrating new programs. One private school at which I taught had very few sports programs and very few students got any exercise at all. The administration was strict on behavior and the kids did their best to behave, but it was clear that their needs for exercise were not being met. Ideas were proposed, but time and money constraints prevented any real change.

The Role of Education in Healthy People and Healthy Economies

Core Principles	Four core approaches to preparing young people include greater utilization of vocational education, teaching personal finance, physical education that supports physical and mental health and the option of daily art class.
Special Education	Helping young people in special education requires steps both inside and outside of the classroom. The core principles are important, but so too is addressing "tracking", walk-to-school programs and building healthy local infrastructure.
Adult Education	Ideally, adult education creates lifelong learners that remain connected to public universities. Perhaps skills can be learned to help rebuild our manufacturing base. Course could be offered that support the mission of the Veterans Conservation Corp.
Chapter Four	Chapter Four offers ways to build local economies that give children opportunities for growth. Walking and bike paths, local farms and parks can all offer valuable lessons.
Chapter Eight	Chapter Eight focuses on ways for universities to promote greener economies through coursework and conservation.

The chart outlines the core attitude of this book, that we need to seize each and every opportunity to improve quality of life for the younger generation both inside and outside of the classroom.

Language Programs

Why are Good Language Programs Important?

Maximizing existing language programs can not only result in greater skill acquisition by students but can grease the wheels for reform in other areas. The good news is that we are quite capable of this.

English Language Skills. Not so long ago I read a report entitled "New Skills for the New Economy," which sought to explain the new skills that were needed in today's market. From the report, it became clear that the new skills were three; some new knowledge of technology, basic math and reading skills and the ability to speak English.

Of the three skill sets, the problem of workers who do not speak English may have the greatest impact. In Massachusetts, there are currently 150,000 workers who speak little or no English, and it limits their ability to provide for themselves and limits their usefulness to employers. (23)

What gives you the authority and experience to talk about improving language progress? Teaching and studying languages for eighteen years at language schools, grammar schools and high schools helped give me clarity about how we can do things better.

Do better language programs need to cost more? No. Although a good supply of "easy readers" can be expensive, more effective programs don't have to cost a lot. In fact, making the class goals specific is half the battle. The main goal I support and with which most should be able to agree is that most students who study a language for four years should be able to speak it.

Good Language Programs Encourage Expression. One important aspect of any language program is to speak in class. Oral drills are good practice, although as teachers at the middle and high school level know, the drills need to be very specific. Most schools don't do many drills in class, which means that students aren't getting enough hands on practice.

How do we get more schools to embrace oral drills in class? One approach to encouraging this expression is to base a large part of the grade on participation. I've known language teachers that base as much as 40% of the grade on this, which is good for learning and promoting a friendly, fun school culture. Basing a good amount of the grade on participation is also more supportive of students with good hearts that may not test well.

How do we assure that workers get what they need to acquire language skills? For ideas on how to improve the English language programs, see the 'Model Language Program' section of this book. Learning to speak English doesn't have to be a lifelong struggle; once specific goals are set, the curriculum follows naturally. The trick is for language teachers to be sharing ideas and feedback on materials. At the college level, focusing on giving struggling adjunct professors the support they need is key. (The issues facing adjunct professors is addressed in depth in the last section of this chapter)

Good Language Programs Means Job Opportunities. As much as the English language continues to spread throughout the world, so too does the value that people place on those that speak the native tongue of any given country. Though English has become increasingly widespread, we're already seeing an increasing insistence on maintenance of the native language and culture. (24) For example, more Germans learning Polish and Poles learning German, as opposed to the two groups strictly learning English.

Useful Cultural Comparisons. Knowing other cultures can help you to better understand your own. I lived in Germany three years and got to know many Germans well. As an American who was earnestly learning their language, my relationship with them was often intensely personal; they were aware of my efforts and as a result they often shared a great deal of themselves. While struggling linguistically (and financially) I also made observations that led to ideas that are featured in this book.

What ideas came from my three years in Germany? The first is the value of testing for university credit (in this chapter) and the second is the German municipal public recreational model explored in Chapter Three.

Good Investments in the Americas? How can language learning help us have better relationships with our neighbors in the Americas? Better job opportunities or more rewarding vacations in South America are just two reasons for us to learn Spanish or Portuguese. Taking the time to learn the language of the host country changes the nature of any visit, as you are showing interest and communicating in the way the natives are most comfortable with. However, there's more to it than fun vacations; we need to be better to our neighbors in the Western Hemisphere. That means investing in a way that benefits the people in the communities where the investment occurs, not just making a quick buck.

What are some signs of South Americans demanding more respect for themselves and the environment? The People's Climate Summit decided to amend the Ecuadorian constitution to include "equal rights to Mother Nature," the continent has lashed back at the abusive behavior of foreign corporations on many fronts. (25) This is good news, in part because it sets the stage for language programs that lead to productive communication between the younger generation in North, Central and South America.

How can we improve K-12 language courses? Above all, the culture has to one in which oral practice can be done well and under control. Students need to learn from a young age how to do oral drills and practice in a fun, relaxed and effective way. If this is learned from a young age, teachers can more easily make the classes more about skill acquisition than only book learning.

How can "language houses" lead to more fun and learning on college campuses? "Language houses" are one cost and time effective way to facilitate skill building and development. These and other ideas are explored in depth in the coming sections; "K-12 Language Study" and "Languages at the Universities."

Our Changing Status. Another argument for better investment in our backyard has everything to do with business; American investments south of the border are no longer the only game in town. Whether we are motivated by altruism or business interests, we need to change our behaviors. "The last 10 years have produced dramatic changes in Latin America…it's no longer the backyard where, either through benign neglect or direct intervention, the US could more or less freely act to achieve its goals," (26) says Miguel Tinker-Salas, a professor of Latin American history at Pomona College in Claremont, Calif.

How do we build better relationships with communities in South America? One aspect of building symbiotic relationships between continents is going to be better communication, and effective study of Spanish and Portuguese can help with that. That doesn't mean that everyone needs to study Spanish, but those that commit four years in high school to learn the language should at least acquire some skills.

The section on languages at the universities promotes the idea of language exchanges via computer, as done by the Tandem Program at the University of Minnesota. (27) Myself high school, I don't see why high school students couldn't do the same thing. This is an interesting opportunity for the next generation of language learners to build friendships across borders!

Integrating Recent Arrivals. Effective English as a Second Language programs can also facilitate smoother integration of recent immigrants, as learning the language can be one of the greatest hurdles to integration. The *MassInc.* publication *New Skills for the New Economy*, better English skills is one of the most needed changes in the Massachusetts workforce. (28) The good news is that our English as a Second Language programs can become more effective with the same changes that will improve our World Language Programs.

Government Jobs. Government agencies can also benefit from Americans learning foreign languages more effectively. The FBI, CIA, Border Patrol and many police departments are always looking for speakers of other languages. (29) Additionally, under new laws many hospitals need to have translators or bilingual staff to speak with patients. Hospitals have difficulty filling these positions, and it is yet another added cost to health care. According to Richard Brecht, "The U.S. education system ... simply has not made the investment in language required to provide the government with an adequate pool of linguistic expertise from which to recruit to meet its needs." (30) Mr. Brecht certainly has a point, which is one more reason for us to college language departments to look at existing, successful models of other departments.

Is there new technology to utilize in language instruction? Again, the "Tandem Plus" programs at the University of Minnesota, where students engage in virtual language exchanges through Skype, is a low cost approach to giving students the practice that they need. I know how effective Skype is for language lessons because I used to get lessons in Chinese this way and am working on tutoring Spanish and German on Skype. In short, it's a great new tool for language learning, exchanges and building relationships.

K-12 Language Study

Seventeen years of experience teaching languages at the grammar, middle and high school level tells me that improving our language programs requires only will, not money. Even better, the process of maximizing language programs can be good for all areas of study and education. Why? It forces us to really talk to and learn from each other, which is a good exercise for finding solutions to other challenges in education.

Language Schools versus High Schools. After teaching English at the *Berlitz* and *Inlingua* language schools in Bonn, Germany I decided to teach high school Spanish. What I found was a vast contrast between the teaching styles at the language schools and those of the high schools. Whereas virtually all students at my language school were progressing visibly from week to week, at the high school the students were putting in a great deal of effort but not learning to speak well. The question is, why? Better books, specific goals, better placement and a classroom culture that can handle oral drills and joyful, natural expression. We need to get away from "busy work" and overemphasis on grammar, then replace it with skill acquisition. However, teachers can't do that alone, they will need the support of administrations to accomplish this.

Methodology; Building the Base. In my professional opinion, the best language teaching method is some form of what I call the "building block method." There are many variations of this, but a typical first lesson uses the ten most basic words and explores every combination of ways to use them together. The next day the teacher might introduce five new words, and drill every combination of using them together. The old words are reinforced while introducing the new, and with each day might come five new words cycled in with the old. Slowly students build a core of the highest frequency words.

What is good news with regards to school language learning? With 183 school days per school year, over the course of four years there are 732 classes for students to build and reinforce their knowledge. With the right system and support for students and teachers, many students should be acquiring a language skill to help them compete in the global marketplace.

Defining Proficiency. Part of the process of making language programs work for students involves understanding what proficiency is. The more clearly we can define this, the easier it is to understand what progress is. At the language schools in which I've taught, level was defined by grammar, vocabulary knowledge and the ability to use both. Reading, writing and speaking are expressions of this knowledge.

How do language schools define full fluency? Full fluency at the Berlitz and other schools is defined as knowledge (at least recognition) of 3000 words and all of the grammar. This is also the number that I arrived at during my years studying languages.

What might be a better attitude regarding fluency? Students don't need to have pressure put on them to perform; they should be able to just enjoy class and their progress. Testing can be informative, but I hate to see test performance become more important than healthy communication in the target language. After all, language learning should be fun and bring students together. Structure is good and can create a learning friendly environment students focus on expressing themselves as well as they can.

Engaging, Effective Expression. Perhaps some recall the scene in the movie The Dead Poets Society in which there was an article on "defining poetry" by Dr. J. Evans Pritchard. (31) In that article students were in practice instructed to use a ruler to measure the poem and its value. That is of course makes no sense. By the same token, the value of expression in any language can't be measured by the amount of grammar or vocabulary mastered.

As one Jiu-Jitsu master who had traveled and trained in Japan put it; "sometimes flashing a thumbs up sign while saying 'excellent' can open all sorts of new doors." So, while this article explores language acquisition in a somewhat scientific way, I haven't forgotten the value of simple yet effective speech. There simply is no substitute for genuine and effective expression, but at the same time the outline of the levels of proficiency that follows can be an effective guide to knowing what a student is capable of. So, let's move on to have a look at the way in which some language schools measure ability.

Levels of Proficiency . During my years of self-study, I used to systematically build my vocabulary and noticed at which points I was able to perform certain tasks, such as reading or listening to the radio.

When I left the U.S. in 1995 to work as an au-pair in Germany, I didn't speak a word of German. I had a little German vocabulary book from the 1950's, which I studied every day for six or seven hours. I counted the number of words in it, and it was about 2,500. What's important is that these were the 2,500 most important words, which make up the vast majority of usage. Over time, I came to have a sense of what was possible with the 100, 500 or 1,000 "highest frequency" words. The good news is that students that can effectively communicate with even the one hundred highest frequency words can say and understand quite a bit. Even better news is that fluency with the one hundred is something the vast majority of students can achieve.

How did teaching at language schools influence your understanding of proficiency "levels?" I remember my first teaching job at the Berlitz School in Bonn in 1995, where they had a description of twelve "language levels" for students. Much of their ability was defined by how much vocabulary they could at least recognize. Seeing that chart was helpful, because it reinforced what I was beginning to believe from my experiences as a learner.

The levels below are designed to serve as a guide as to what is possible when learning a language with specific levels of vocabulary and grammar. There is no substitute for a friendly person with a good heart that's trying their best to communicate in another language, but the (admittedly dry) measures below can be helpful.

Level 1 Students have recognition of up to 500 highest frequency words and basic grammar. The ability to use even the one hundred highest frequency words fluently makes conversation possible, something any high school students that study a language for four years should be able to do.

Level 2 At least recognition of the core 500–1000 words, along with the most functional intermediate grammar. The post-World War Two German Chancellor Konrad Adenauer had an English vocabulary of about 600–700 words, but was able to talk comfortably with English speaking heads of state. Reaching this level is a good goal for high school students.

Level 3 At least recognition of vocabulary of 1000–1500 words, most verb tenses and intermediate grammar. At this level you should be able to read some articles and understand most television programs.

Level 4 Students in level four have recognition of the 1500-2000 highest frequency words. Novels and magazines are very readable, even if 5-6 words per page are unknown.

Level 5 Vocabulary of 2000–2500 words and most advanced grammar. The student should be able to read newspapers and books, although literature and editorials may still be tough.

Level 6 Students should at least recognize the 2500–3000 highest frequency words and most grammar. The stories in the highest level books of the first language school I taught at were written using the 3,000 highest frequency words..

Supporting English Language Learners. The ramifications of this chart are big for learners of English as a Second Language. This is important; because according to *MassInc.* (the original core source of this book), in my home state of Massachusetts 150,000 adults aged 18-64 speak little or no English. (32) The good news is that seventeen years of teaching languages has taught me that with a systematic approach, English language learners can advance much more rapidly. After living in Germany for three years as an immigrant, I understand the stresses and challenges that make learning the new language hard. However, I also know that with the right textbooks and a system learning English can be much easier. Additionally, the Internet means that more learners can find language exchange partners online and exchange through Skype.

Effective Textbooks. Teachers need to have the best learning materials to assure that hard working students are acquiring skills in the language they've chosen to study. However, in my experience, most of the middle and high school textbooks don't incorporate anything that resembles what I call "the building block method." Too often it seems that the goal is just to get through the book, not to actually teach students skills. In my opinion, we owe it to students to give them books that enable true skill acquisition, not just keep them busy.

What is the challenge with getting better textbooks? Firstly, there are limited subject assessment tests in the schools; with no common assessment of what has been learned there is less drive to make textbooks effective. Secondly, contracts between school systems and textbook companies are reportedly quite political, and changing books involves more than just looking for the best methodology. Thirdly, very few people are aware of the methods used in some language schools and by serious language learners.

The Importance of Reading. Reading helps language learning because it allows the learner to see the words and grammar in play. The challenge for beginning students is to find appropriate readings. Ideally, as in the language schools, the teacher is aware of what vocabulary the students are supposed to have, and has corresponding readings. If the teacher can manage to bring the students up to a vocabulary of about 250, then there are appropriate books that can be bought.

Does any institution carry this sort of easy reader? For example, if you go into the *French Library of Boston* and tell the librarian you're looking for some easy readers, she'll lead you to an area that has 250's, 500's or 750's. That is, books that are based on 250, 500 or 750 highest frequency words.

Why are "easy readers" so valuable to students with low vocabulary? They can gain the benefit of reading; reviewing core words and grammar while getting a better feel for the language. For many, reading is the stepping stone to speaking and understanding the language well. If more school language programs could organize their readings in accordance with this system, the students could benefit greatly.

What is another existing equivalent of step by step reading programs? The SRA. When I was in grammar school, we did a portion of English class together separately, during which time we'd focus on reading. Everyone did readings appropriate to their level with reading comprehension questions. We would start at the low level readings, and if we could answer the comprehension questions we would move on to the next level-yellow, blue or whatever. Today, computer programs in the language lab are an equivalent program for foreign languages; students can all be at their own work station and do readings with questions at their own level.

Language Assessment. Effective assessment tests are another key element to assure students are acquiring skills in World Language classes. In order to raise standards there has to be a standard, and good assessment can help to assure that students who study a language for four years can actually speak it. In my professional opinion this is only fair to students.

How do subject assessment tests help with learning languages? Employers and colleges need to have some idea what skill level is meant by an "A" or a "B" on school report cards. With a quality assessment system, everyone will know that all material taught in the classroom will be on a subject assessment test eventually. Whether students take Advanced Placement tests, subject assessment tests or use computer programs, good assessment can help everyone know how much is being learned.

What is one part of the "test culture" you don't like? I don't like young people being under too much pressure and I also don't like putting a priority on test scores above all else, such as how much they contribute to the class. That said, doing well on a test should mean that a young person has acquired some skills. Hard working students deserve a curriculum that will help them students acquire a skill and be able to converse.

Placement. One of the most important aspects of any language program is appropriate placement. Students in a second language class should want to be there. That's not to say that language classes have to be an elitist club — in my professional opinion a foreign language in high school is a good idea for 70–80% of students.

Why is it important for language classes to be a choice? Time in the classroom is valuable. If students aren't up to doing the work involved in a quality language class then they should find an activity they like better. At the grammar school level everyone should get a chance to try out foreign language study and see if they like it, but at the high school level it should be an informed decision.

The Participation Grade. Making participation a large part of the final grade can encourage students to do a better job speaking and helping other students do the same. In my experience, teachers vary from basing between ten to forty percent of the total grade on participation. And although there are many variables that go into choosing this number, I believe that a higher percentage of the grade being based on participation can help to improve classroom culture. Firstly, it encourages students to speak and practice the language that they've chosen. Secondly, it allows good students the opportunity to help out the weaker students, which is good for school culture.

Languages at the Universities

All college students can benefit from effective language studies at the universities, from language majors to students with a casual interest to those just looking to acquire a skill. In this section we're looking at some of the same ideas on language learning, applied at the college level.

What is similar and what is different about college language courses? Those ways are the same ones I'm always going on about; better books, language school style goals and proficiency testing.

At the college level there are a few to look at; more test preparation for future teachers, language houses and testing for credit. Last but not least, language departments have a great deal to learn from each other, which is why some are profiled in the next section.

Realistic Syllabuses. In my experience, the syllabuses in college foreign language literature courses are often way too ambitious. For example, one French literature course assigned reading six or seven full books in French. Maybe one or two of the graduate students in the course might have been able to handle the reading, but for most of us it was just too much. Most of us would have been much better off reading one or two chapters of one book per week. That way we could have time to truly understand and digest all of the material.

At the same time, how often does the extensive literary knowledge of professors go untapped because students are struggling just to understand the basics of the language? And what can we do about this? For starters, we can improve this situation with an upgrade of the goals and learning materials in the K-12 system.

Testing for Credit. One idea I've thought about a lot is testing for university credit. As it stands, if a student can pass an Advanced Placement exam in a language with a 3, 4 or 5, some colleges get the equivalent of one college course credit. The question is whether this could be expanded upon to help raise standards while making education more affordable.

At most American Universities, which rely on tuition to function, there is no such exam. It is understandable that private colleges would be against testing for credit if it would reduce revenues, but public universities exist to serve the people. Although many colleges may offer testing for credit, a casual search revealed that the *University of Iowa* offers credit in three ways; through the Advanced Placement program, the International Baccalaureate Program and the College Level Examination Program. (33)

I don't have the time to be looking at the details of individual programs and how they do or don't serve the general good, but researching this might make for some very good, useful books.

How can testing for credit options at state colleges serve the poor well? Along with affordable state colleges, testing for credit could work for those with no money to pay for pricey private colleges. If built upon, it could help revive town centers as places of learning and to live out one Massachusetts' poet's dream of "making every village a university." Imitating systems such as the Tandem Plus in Iowa, groups of adults who meet for classes could begin to work together to acquire skills for life.

Teachers and the System. Future middle and high school language teachers could benefit from college programs that more effectively track proficiency. I have known too many teachers who majored in French or Spanish but yet still struggle to speak and read it comfortably. We can fix this.

In Massachusetts, all public school teachers have to pass a certification exam; one general literacy test and one test for his or her area of specialization. The exams for Spanish and other languages are difficult and many don't pass it the first time. Many colleges help future teachers by providing courses that meet some of the other certification requirements. If colleges could take the necessary steps to improve preparing students for the language teaching certification exams, they would be doing many future teachers a great service.

College Language Houses. "Language houses" on our college campuses where students can live and work with others to reach their language learning goals is a large, often untapped opportunity for students to build skills. Considering that the cost of housing is more than tuition at some colleges, greater utilization of "program housing" only makes sense. It's not just about the facilities; houses or parts of a dormitory hall with a few determined learners can be enough for fun and to create opportunity for advancement.

What's my personal experience with "language houses?" I remember the German House at Wesleyan University (34) in Middletown Connecticut; those people had a blast living and reaching their together. Students not only encouraged each other in their skill acquisition, but they practiced and learned to work together with all kinds of house members.

In my experience, at the end of the day that's what people want; to work and connect with other people, to reach goals together.

University and Government Cooperation. The 2003 International Studies in Higher Education Act began an era of the government giving money to university language programs, the idea being to "reflect national needs related to Homeland Security." Harvard University was one recipient of this money, with the Center for Middle Eastern Studies receiving $275,000 annually. The Asia Center receives $433,000 annually and the David Rockefeller Center for Latin American Studies was receiving an average of $433,333 a year. (35)

What was the nature of cuts instituted in 2011? Funding to Harvard University was cut significantly, but the government money flowing to the private college is still significant. (36) It might it be more fruitful and fair to spread the money around to multiple programs, in particular to state university language programs that struggle just to maintain a basic level of coursework.

Why is it good to spread the money around? In the meantime, colleges looking to both add value to their programs and perhaps become more worthy of funding can read about some of the existing, successful models profiled in the next section.

Language Learning Models & Materials. Maximizing our university language learning programs can be a fun, cathartic process for the simple fact that there are so many successful models out there to learn from. Here we have existing programs or materials that exemplify some of the fundamentals of successful learning outlined in the previous section. As a language teacher, it was very educational to research this section. Imitating these successful programs doesn't necessarily have to cost much; even affordable state colleges (powerful assets in these times) can learn from and apply these ideas.

Systematic Vocabulary Building . College programs work hard to assure that students are building vocabulary systematically, although I like the approach of the Colorado State German professor, who does it by assigning twenty-five to thirty word compositions. This is a good way to assure the "core word repetitions" that students need to build the base to comfortably communicate. (37)

How do we engage the critical thinking skills as well? Asking students to be creative also means engaging more of their brain, which increases the value of the assignment. The 25-30 daily essay length is also a good, modest length for beginners, which allows them to focus on writing correctly.

The Role of Frequency Dictionaries. For the record, I find that the single best system for building vocabulary is through the Routledge "Frequency Dictionaries." A frequency dictionary is a book that lists words in the order of frequency in which they appear in a language.

What is the first step? So, if you learn words 1-100, you will have mastered the one hundred most common words, or perhaps about 30% of usage. In this way learners assure that they are learning words they will need.

Effective Easy Readers. In eighteen years of teaching languages I have used many different materials and found a few books that worked particularly well. I'm not being paid to endorse any brand; I'm only sharing a few products that have worked well.

Why were the Berlitz Materials so effective? The first were the books at the *Berlitz School*, where I had my first teaching job in Bonn, Germany in 1995. They were effective because they introduced a small amount of new material and reviewed the old with reading, writing and speaking. Each and every lesson had some readings that used only words that the students had been taught. With beginners, this is the key; providing simple stories that can help them succeed.

So, if you can't buy the Berlitz books, then what series of easy readers do you like? The second series of books that really worked were those of the Blaine Ray, including *Pobre Ana* and *Ana Va a California*. As you may know, one of the best things to do for your language studies is to read, but the hard part is to get your vocabulary up to the point where it's possible. The Blaine Ray series have books and stories with controlled vocabularies, so you only need to know about three hundred words to begin to read, as opposed to most "easy readers" which require a vocabulary of about six hundred words.

What is a college language programs that has rich content and advanced use technology? One example is Spanish 311 at the College of Wooster, where Spanish playwrights make regular performances - - digitally.

They also do face to face and class to class exchanges through Skype. Called "Contemporary Spanish Theatre in a Global Context," the model opens up many new doors, including adding a whole new dimension to "sister cities" and classrooms. (38)

Why do communities in Central and South America need to really pay attention to relationships with foreigners? As communities in South America struggle to preserve natural resources and unique ways of life, there are always challenges. It's not the purpose of this section of the book to discuss public policy so much as the value of young people learning and communicating? Connections between classrooms north and south of the border can facilitate communication and friendship between members of the younger generation.

Why are language exchanges so unique and valuable? Partnering with another student to practice languages is one of the best ways to progress, have fun and bring the language alive. However, not everyone meets such a partner during the college years, which is why someone needs to facilitate these exchanges.

What is a good model for language partner facilitation? The University of Minnesota "Tandem Plus' program is one. (39) They organize three kinds of exchanges' face-to-face, virtual face-to –face and class-to-class. Official policy states that "priority is given to language students currently enrolled in a class at the University of Minnesota, but registration is open to all." So, is there was difficult finding an exchange partner for a student studying a more rarely studied language, (Urdu, Farsi or Swahili, for example) then perhaps someone could be found in the community for such an exchange. At the end of the day, what makes the TandemPlus program worth imitating is the low cost and high return.

What is a good example of a college language house? The Reed College Program House "language houses" are places where students can live and work together while speaking a foreign language can support effective learning, and Reed College has a good model for this. Every fall, eight so-called "language scholars" come or return to the college to act as mentors to students in the language program houses. So, regardless of which of the five languages that students elect to study, there is a house where students can live and practice the language they're working on. (40)

How can we improve language teacher preparation? For students that intend to become teachers themselves, they might consider taking the teacher's certification test in the language they intend to teach in their junior year. In the event they don't pass, they can use test feedback to prepare for the next exam. At Salem State University, they have an "MTEL Center," a place where students get help preparing for Massachusetts teacher certification exams.

The MTEL Center or other teacher test preparation centers could be greatly assisted in their mission of preparing future language teachers by integrating ideas profiled here; better books, exchanges and language houses. With student learning being promoted in all these dynamic ways, the centers can focus more on tactics for students to pass the test itself, because the material has more likely been learned well.

Cross Listing of Language Courses. A casual search on Google for a language department that integrates language learning coursework with other disciplines brought the University of Indiana to the top of the page. (41) Their web site offered at least part of what I was looking for; a web page (see end note) and program that allows for applying credit from other departments. Cross listing just might create a new group highly motivated to acquire a new skill.

Adult Education

Many Americans feel the decline of the sense of community. Whether it's the loss of hometown manufacturing jobs, longer commutes, increased average work hours or the spread of crime, many neighborhoods now have struggling schools and economies. Quality adult education, combined with utilizing the local economy ideas outlined in Chapter Four can give struggling adults a much needed boost.

Adult Education. There are three main areas of adult education; remedial education, English language acquisition and courses in the community. Remedial education often involves building basic language and reading skills, while English language courses are all about acquiring skills in English, obviously. What's relevant here is to share some core information and highly successful approaches to these subject areas. (42)

How can community-based learning revitalize towns and cities? One way to improve the importance of adult programs could be through the introduction of testing for credit. The University of Iowa has a system other states might consider, a system by which there are three ways to receive university credit. (43) The relevance of this to community is that state universities might connect to local learning, thereby encourage life-long learners and skill-building.

How might the system of testing for credit interface with local economies? Community-based courses could be revolutionized if the state universities offered tests that could be taken for credit. Adults could then work together as a group toward a particular goal and make their own small town a center of learning and advancement.

Struggling Adjunct Professors. One of the less publicized issues in education is the fact that many college adjunct professors are struggling to survive and put food on the table for their children.

Why is there a focus on supporting adjunct professors? By marginalizing adjunct professors and and allowing them to become one more downtrodden group in this country we are marginalizing a group that is a large part of the backbone of college student learning. If we can succeed in improving their situation we are finding ways to improve the situation of America's working poor. According to the *LA Times*, adjuncts have large teaching loads, are poorly paid, often have to share cramped office space and get no health insurance. (44) Another article was more damning, saying that research came out "showing that most adjunct professors work at poverty or near-poverty wages, as well as several high-profile stories detailing homelessness, lack of health insurance, and death among their ranks." (45) Readers should understand the injustice of this; the next step is to understand how this has a wider negative effect.

How do poor working conditions of adjunct professors affect student learning? According to an article in the *Chronicle for Higher Education*, if adjuncts have "a lack of access to personal office space, computers, library resources, and curriculum guidelines, among other things, and "the education experience of students suffers, both inside and outside of the classroom." (46) In another quote from that same article, Maria Maisto, the President of the New Faculty Majority said; "Faculty working conditions are student learning conditions, but we realize that people don't get that connection." (47) In short, adjuncts need the resources to feel their best and contribute positively to student learning.

What ideas in this book can help the situation of adjunct professors? Steps forward in Chapters Five could help adjunct professors through coming up with a plan to protect Social Security in the long run. Chapter Three; "Creating Opportunities for the Common Man" offers a few ideas on how those with limited incomes can survive and thrive, whereas Chapter Seven highlights approaches to building health.

What is Working Already

Walk to School Programs

What is the role of walk-to-school programs at grammar schools? The idea is for children to get enough exercise to focus in their learning environment. The national group *Safe Routes* has had successes in virtually every state helping to build new walking paths or utilizing existing resources. You can check out their interactive map to learn about successful programs near you.

What benefits do walk-to-school programs have on children? According to the national group *Safe Routes*, walking to school can help children relax and feel better in their working environment, "build a sense of neighborhood and encourage increased parental involvement at school & beyond." (48) Using the interactive map, you can read about success stories on the Safe Routes website, saferoutesinfo.org.

What does my community need to do to make walking and bike paths happen? Two approaches include a grant from *Safe Routes* or the creation of "local experts," people who know their community intimately and who have had training on the implementation of these paths, as prescribed by the PBIC; the Pedestrian, Bike and Information Center. For that to happen, colleges near you need to offer the coursework prescribed by the PBIC. (49)

Do you see the walk-to-school programs advocated in this book as being a substitute for physical education? No, but they're part of the whole picture. The programs sponsored by *Safe Routes* help students find walking routes to school, but I would hope that they don't preclude the perceived need for physical education. By utilizing their interactive map you can click on a state and read about existing programs near you.

Healthier School Lunches

Are there any existing, successful examples of healthy good school food? The best thing seems to defer to an expert on healthy food for young people – Jamie Oliver. As the young Brit said; "This food revolution is about saving American's health by changing the way they eat...if you care about your kids and their future, take this revolution and make it your own." (50) Does this mean that Jamie Oliver has all the answers? No, but his website offers models for people to learn from.

Are there existing, successful models on healthy school food that could help students in special education? Yes. One example of bringing healthy food back into the schools is the work of Jamie Oliver, who has led the reintroduction of quality food in the schools in England. (51) A second existing, successful model about the value of serving better food in schools was the French movie *Food Beware: The French Organic Revolution.* The French title "Nos enfants nous accuseront" or "*Our Children Accused Us*" is, in French fashion, a bit more blunt. (52)

Integrating Education and Quality of Life Points

Core Education Principles	Greater utilization of vocational education, teaching the basics of personal finance, healthy school lunches and physical education that supports health is a start.
Chapter Eight Concepts	Chapter Eight; Winning the Green Revolution on college campuses is about creating problem-solvers, healers and people to build up our walking and bike paths, create green jobs and with it reinvent the college experience.
New Authors, Journalists and Colleges	We need hundreds of new authors, journalists and college classrooms to sink their teeth into the issues in this book with their heart. Then we will see true progress.

Of course the chart above raises as many questions as it answers. Questions to ask include; How do we go about exploring the creation of healthy school lunches on a budget? Should daily physical education be an option? How can physical education be used to help girl's maintain and build their self-esteem to withstand cruel social pressures? What role can healthy local farms play in providing summer jobs for students? What role can school newspapers play in building a healthier culture? Do we apply these ideas differently in rich suburban towns than less affluent communities?

. . .

Chapter One Questions

1. What are five core areas to be looked at to maximize the role of education?

2. What do you think of doing a combination of traditional and vocational studies? Is this feasible in your hometown school system? Why or why not?

3. Do you agree with the idea of minimum standard tests? How is their role different from subject assessment tests?

4. I once had a professor who flat out didn't believe in testing; what's your reaction to that?

5. Do you agree that physical education should be a daily requirement? What are the laws in your state regarding this? How are they enforced? Are there any loopholes?

6. Did the section on Special Education give you any feeling of hope or optimism? Was there any particular point you found useful?

7. Which idea for maximizing physical programs would best be integrated into the schools?

8. Was there any point or idea in the section on Adult Education that you liked?

9. What did you think about the idea of "Language Houses" at our state universities?

10. In your opinion, how should adjunct professors go about improving their situation?

2

Keeping the American Dream Alive

"Over the last 30 years, there has been an unprecedented growth in income inequality. Eighty percent of Americans have seen their wages diminish or stagnate. Now it takes two wage earners in a family to make the equivalent of what one used to earn."

-Mark Erlich, Executive Secretary-Treasurer, New England Council of Carpenters (1)

The world is changing and so is the State of the American dream; we all know that. Longer work hours and commutes, high housing and health care costs have contributed to the decline in health and quality of life for many Americans. This chapter is a response to the situation; we look at the specifics of some of these changes and how they affect the different economic groups and follow up by looking at strategies to adapt.

Everyone can benefit from good green infrastructure; both the process of building it and the glorious results. We will look into how to build the tools to *know how* to improve our network of walking and bike paths and national parks. In my opinion, we should explore moving defense spending to investment in national parks, ideally facilitated by the *Veterans Conservation Corps*. Why? What better than hiring veterans to maintain and expand our natural resources while giving much needed employment?

At the end of the day, the goal is to find ways to maximize quality of life, despite how difficult the situation may or may not be.

Chapter Two Concerns

A. TIME BANKING AND THE LOCAL ECONOMY.-Introduce the time banking model and analyze what it can do for business owners, families and especially elderly people. Then, reflect how it interacts with other aspects of the local economy.

B. RECENT TRENDS AND THE FIVE QUINTILES-Look at how the five economic groups of 20% (quintiles) are affected by changes in 1) increased work hours, 2) the changing role of high school, 3) more necessary and expensive universities, 4) increased crime and 5) declining physical and mental health. After using five criteria to assess the situation of different economic groups, the chapter offers solutions for improving the situation of each economic group. That's to say that the solutions proposed for discussion are tailor made for each group. There is room for hundreds of authors to further develop and explore these suggestions, but they're a good start.

. . .

Time Banking and Local Economy

What is time banking? Time banking is built around the concept of measuring work in terms of hours, not dollars. Everyone's skills, whether they are a medical professional or a house painter, are worth one "time dollar" per hour. The hours that you earn are stored in a "time bank" and can then be redeemed for any service of your choice from any member of the time bank. Whereas barter is between two people, hours earned through a time bank exchange can be used to "buy" services from any member of the group.

The world's first time bank was created by Teruko Mizushima in 1973, utilizing ideas she had been developing since the 1940's. She foresaw that members might contribute when they were less busy and take back time later when they needed it. She also saw it as a method to deal with challenges associated with an ageing society. In the U. S in 1992, Edgar Cahn published the first of his books; "Time Dollars; the New Currency that Enables Americans to Turn Their Hidden Resource-Time-into Personal Security and Community Renewal." It was in part through that book that time banking was introduced to the U.S..

What kinds of services might you offer? Very often they are services that don't exist in the market economy, such as an hour's worth of help in your garden or helping an older person set up an e-mail account. Time banking is simply about spending an hour doing something for somebody in your community. That hour goes into the Time Bank as a Time Dollar you can spend on having someone do something for you. (2) Hypothetical; if a carpenter works twenty paid hours a week and struggles to pay his bills, he might choose to work about five hours a week and earn "time dollars" that he can use on services for his family and home.

How does time banking relate to quality of life for members of different economic groups? Everyone has something to offer and everyone gets value back from the time bank in their own way. Perhaps the most important principle is that through the system of time banks, *everyone* has something to give. At the "Hour World" is an interactive map to find a time bank near you. Below you can see services time banks offer outside the market that can help everyone.

Table 2.1 "Non-Market" Services and Benefits of Time banks

Community Building Events	Emotional Support for Bullying Victims (3)	Language Exchanges
Garden Help	Companionship for Elderly	Emotional Support for Trauma
Resume Coaching	Odd Jobs	Parental Listening and Support
Peer Tutoring	Support Services for the Deaf and Blind	Storytelling

What was time banking originally designed for? Although the time bank model was originally designed for senior care, (4) you can see in the chart above that the scope of services most time banks offer has expanded considerably.

What role do time banks play in the local economy? Time banks are one "spoke in the wheel" of local economies. In other words, a time bank can play a powerful role in tandem with investing in local banks, shared housing, Community Supported Agriculture, farmer's markets, walking and bike infrastructure and co-ops. We will look at the level of need for local economy initiatives for the different economic groups in the next section, whereas Chapter Four explores these themes in depth. That said the good news is that everyone can contribute to quality of life in new, local economies.

What's the best place to learn more about time banks and other local economy ventures? You can check out the site of *Hour World* or to find a time bank near you. To find local farms near you, check out the website "Local Harvest."

Recent Trends and the Five Quintiles

The coming paragraphs look at how a variety of socio-economic factors have influenced quality of life of the different economic groups. All economic groups are working more hours, paying more for college and suffering from higher levels of stress and depression. However, both the specifics of the changes and the recommended responses for each group are a bit different. We'll start with some statistics for the lowest economic twenty percent.

The Lowest Earning 20%

When talking about the effect of change on the lower middle economic twenty percent we're talking about Americans that probably have a full time job but most certainly have areas of their life that have room for improvement. I've done my best to connect the different chapters and point out opportunities for this group, but I'm just one guy trying his best; you may find themes from Chapters One, Three, Seven or Eight that are a better match to those in this economic group that need help.

Increased Work Hours for the Lowest Earning 20%

Between 1979 and 1999, income for the lowest earning economic quintile group decreased in real income terms from $11,767 to $10,341. Top book responses to this situation include greater utilization of vocational education to creating a skilled workforce, as discussed in Chapter One Second, we need to create local economy jobs, as outlined in Chapter Four.

Average Work Hours Families in this bracket worked an average of 1100 hours a year, or about 22 hours a week. The average hourly wage was $7.29 per hour. During this same time, the percentage of hours worked by women in this group went from 12% to 30% of total earnings. The increase in work hours by women in this group seems to be the result of necessity, not want. (5) For a very short but thought provoking video on the subject of poverty and the struggles of unemployment, former presidential candidate Robert Reich did a good one called "The War on the Poor and Working Families." (6)

Why is vocational education so important to creating jobs? Greater utilization of vocational education can create a skilled workforce to rebuild our manufacturing base. In my home state of Massachusetts, only seven percent of students utilize vocational education, although according to *MassInc.* that number should be around thirty to forty percent., with as many as fifty percent doing a combination of traditional and vocational studies.

What are local economy responses to create employment in this bracket? Thriving local economies, including co-ops, local farms and a robust network of walking and bike paths can assure the availability of some jobs. Time banking can help the elderly poor give and receive essential services, make friends and find partners to set and reach health goals with. To stop the suffering of elderly poverty, emphasis needs to be placed on securing and maximizing Social Security, the core theme of Chapter Five.

Why is it important to build up our network of walking and bike paths? Transportation costs make up a large part of the budget for low income people, which is why we need more access to walking and biking options. Using the tools on the website pedbikeinfo.org and the models of the national group *Safe Routes,* we can create high quality walking and bike options for everyone.

How might increased investment in the Veterans Conservation Corp help veterans in poverty? The *Veterans Conservation Corp.* employs returning veterans in conservation projects, which both helps veterans make the adjustment to civilian life and funds conservation projects that improve public resources. Moving a large amount defense spending to this organization would be a huge win for national parks, veterans and the communities they live in. Instead of more Americans dying overseas we could begin to support existing veterans properly. Second, those working hard to expand our national park system need support; the existence of a pool of returning heroes to assist in those efforts would be a great boon to them and the communities their efforts serve.

High School Education and the Lowest Earning 20%

The schools had their share of challenges in 1979, but at that time it was arguably easier to build a life on a high school education. As of 1999, 35 percent of people in this group were without a high school education, 36.7 had a high school diploma and 5.2% had a college degree. The statistics are from 1999 but clearly show the relationship between education and income.

Table 2.2 Academic Achievement by Income Level (6)

	1-20%	21-40%	41-60%	61-80%	81-100%
Bachelor	5.2	9.9	16.3	25.5	33.5
Masters or Higher	1.9	3.4	6.7	13.2	27.7

Why is education especially important for those of low incomes? Because the diploma they get and what they learn in school might be all they have. As Bill Murray said about the rich boys in the movie Rushmore; (to the supreme excitement of Max Fisher) "for some of you it doesn't matter; you were born rich and you're going to stay rich....just remember; they can buy anything but they can't buy backbone. Don't let them forget that." This is why greater utilization of vocational education and teaching personal finance are so critical.

How can time outside the classroom be maximized? First, the walk-to-school programs promoted by the group *Safe Routes* can help students get exercise and be more relaxed in their learning environment. Second, serving healthy, locally grown food can help children feel better and be great for the local economy. Models for serving healthy food on a budget can be found at the website of the British chef Jamie Oliver, who has made it his business to increase the quality of school food.

Are there a disproportionate number of children from low income families in Special Education? Unfortunately, yes. There are multiple causes of this, but one is the problem of child hunger. After watching the movie *A Place at the Table*, I learned that hunger in school not an isolated incident, and that in fact 16% of children in Americans face "food insecurity."

Responding to child hunger requires a multi-faceted approach, from better school lunches, supporting local farms and making high quality food more available. British chef Jamie Oliver is one of a number of people that have made fighting this issue a priority. Another movie on the subject is the French film "*Les Enfants Nous Accuseront*." The theme of healthy food is in Chapter Four.

Is "tracking" especially relevant to low-income families? Yes. Students from low-income families are often stuck in one level, feel stigmatized and work alone on rote work sheets. The tragedy is that what disenfranchised children need is the exact opposite; work with peers, problem- solving assignments in groups and rich, relevant content. Good articles on tracking that go into this in great depth include "The Case for Tracking" by Anne Wheelock and "On Tracking and Individual Differences; A Conversation with Jeannie Oakes" by John O'Neil.

In short, there are many obstacles for the poor to overcome to get the kind of education they need to succeed, which is the reason that this book advocates attacking issues in education from every side. Looking at tracking is good, as is greater utilization of vocational education, teaching personal finance as part of math class, school lunches that serve locally grown food and other ideas that are developed in depth in Chapter One. The ideas in Chapter Four on local economies are also relevant, because healthy local economies can give children opportunities to learn and grow.

Opportunities at Universities for the Lowest Earning 20%

Among other things, Table 2.2 demonstrates just how large a role a college education can play in making more money, which of course means more parents have to concern themselves with paying for it. Below are some thoughts and statistics on affordable college options.

Public vs. Private Public colleges are far more affordable than their private counterparts. In 2011-12, public four-year colleges charge, on average, $8,244 in annual tuition and fees for in-state students. The average surcharge for full-time out-of-state students at public state institutions is $12,526. By contrast, private nonprofit four-year colleges charge, on average, $28,500 per year in tuition and fees. (7)

What are some affordable college options? According to the College Board; "In 2011-12, 44 percent of all full-time undergraduate college students attend a four-year college that has published charges of less than $9,000 per year for tuition and fee. At two-year colleges, the average price for tuition and fees is $2,963. As the College Board says; "learn about the two-year college experience." (8) Also, an article in Yahoo reports that a number of private colleges are cutting tuition. (9) So, there are options. I should also add that Chapter Eight advocates tactics to add value to the experience on campus, as well as to quality of life for those of all incomes. With a healthier, greener lifestyle promoted on our campuses, rich and poor should be able to access healthy food and the wonders of our natural resources.

Crime in the Neighborhoods of the Lowest Economic Twenty Percent

Social theorists can argue about whether or not the poor (who are part of this group) or more or less likely to commit crime, but that discussion isn't interesting to me. What is of concern is how much the innocent are affected by the crime rate. As you can see from the statistics below, the number of all reported offenses in the country (violent and property crimes) spiked from 1960 to 1990, almost quadrupling. (10)

Year	Population	Total Offenses
1960	179 million	3,338,200
1970	203 million	8,098,000
1991	252 million	14,872,000
2001	284 million	11,849,006

What is some good work we can do for those suffering in prison or in danger of going there? To start, it's important to be aware at an empathetic level of many of the injustices of our system. For that I recommend the movie *Gideon's Army*, which profiles the lives of those who defend those who can't defend themselves. Second, prisons might offer courses in personal finance to help inmates better adjust to life on the outside. Third, each and every step we can take to make our neighborhoods healthier and happy places can help; ideas to that end are outlined in Chapter Four.

How can we make neighborhoods safer? One approach is to increase the level of homeownership and one avenue worth exploring is shared home ownership, through which people can build capital and pay a small mortgage as opposed to paying high rent. However, before this can be a viable option there is a great deal of legal work to be done, including work by lawyers to build better contracts, ones that protect all parties involved.

In the words of the Neighborhood Reinvestment Corporation; "Home ownership helps communities with public benefits such as increased tax revenues, greater private investment, and stronger and safer neighborhoods." (11) In the words of The Ohio State University professor Robert Dietz; "Homeownership confers social benefits to individuals and communities due to the unique bundle of characteristics that are associated with home ownership. These characteristics include a financial stake in the dwelling and its neighborhood." (12) In short, communities with a high percentage of home owners have more people invested in the safety and well-being of the area.

Might co-ownership contribute to greater well-being for returning veterans, especially those with Post Traumatic Stress Disorder (PTSD)? Possibly, if a lot of lawyers do some good work building contracts that protect people. The viability of this system for struggling veterans should be explored by college classrooms and local papers alike; not only for the financial benefits but also for the value of having roommates and co-owners to work and share their struggles with. Ideally, this system will be combined with significant investment in the *Veterans Conservation Corp.*, a program that provides veterans with employment in conservation projects. This program is a triple win; 1) Veterans get work that can be good for their often suffering soul, 2) communities benefit from the presence of our defenders in peace building projects and 3) Conservation projects get the support they need.

Table 2.3 Mortgage Payments for Multiple Payers on a 30 Year Mortgage

Loan	1 Payer	2 Payers	3 Payers	4 Payers
100,000	600	300	200	150
200,000	1200	600	400	300

Note: The numbers are a ballpark figure for a thirty year mortgage and do not include taxes or insurance.

Do you know anyone who has experimented with co-ownership? Yes. Five friends that went to Boston College bought an apartment together after graduation. They had the time of their lives together and as they got married and sold off their shares of the apartment, until eventually one guy remained with whom eventually became his wife. There was one guy who created problems when he backed out of the deal, and this is one risk in such an arrangement. There are also many other potential complications, which is why lawyers, real estate agents and community activists need to work together on creating really good contracts that can protect buyers.

Building Health for the Lowest Income 20%

Before talking about building health for this group we'll look at two statistics on anxiety and depression for the general population. These are huge numbers, and clearly economics, quality of food, access to green space and healthy activity are factors.

1. 40 million Americans (out of a population of 310 million) will experience an impairment because of an anxiety condition this year. Only 4 million will receive treatment for stress and of those only 400,000 will receive proper treatment.

2. 65% of Americans take prescription medications daily, 43% take mood altering prescriptions daily. (13)

Do people of low-incomes suffer more than others? Experience, common sense and the research says yes. Gary Evans, a professor of human ecology at Cornell University wrote; "There's a lot more demands on low-income families. We know that produces stress in families, including on the children," (14) Evans said. This is why we need to explore every idea that can improve quality of life for this group.

Can higher quality food help stress and depression? I think so. As Hippocrates said; "Let thy food be thy medicine and thy medicine be thy food." In the movie *A Place at the Table* I learned that increasing the quality of food is especially important for poorer neighborhoods because of so-called "food deserts"; poorer neighborhoods where there is a lack of fresh, healthy food in the stores. This is where dynamic local economies come in; not only can they awaken an often stagnant national job market, but food from local farms can improve the health of children if it is served in the cafeteria.

What changes can we make in education to create happier, more balanced students? With a disproportionately high number of poor in special education, education policies are relevant. Articles by field experts suggest that what all learners need is what many students from poor families in special education aren't getting; content rich material, working with peers and group activities.

Whereas the current tendency within the system of tracking is for students to work alone with worksheets, experts say we have to do the opposite and bring studies alive with problem-solving and activities with peers.

What is the role of education in building health of children at school? Walk-to-school programs, healthy lunches, daily physical education and art can all go a long way to make the school day more productive and fun. Additionally, I believe that engaging the younger generation in conservation and expansion of our park systems could bring science class alive and help the next generation to take better care of our world. This theme is explored in depth in Chapter Eight.

As for healthy school lunches, British Chef Jamie Oliver said it best; "Imagine a world where children were fed tasty and nutritious, real food at school from the age of 4 to 18. A world where every child was educated about how amazing food is, where it comes from, how it affects the body and how it can save their lives." You can read about Chef Oliver at his website, jamieoliver.com.

What is the role of Social Security for low income people? We need to build a long-term plan for securing Social Security and exploring ways for Americans to maximize their benefits. This is the theme of Chapter Five; "Securing Social Security," a theme that local papers and new authors should address through a series of workshops, roundtables and discussions within communities.

What is an utterly far out idea that would be fun to explore and make happen, one that could reduce the stress of the poor? We could build walking and bike paths alongside our highways. As a Massachusetts resident, I use Route 128 more than any other highway and I dream of the day when we can build walking and bike paths alongside that road. Think of the all the federal money that went into the stimulus package or money spent on war; that money could certainly pay for *at least stretches of road* where these paths existed. Personally, I believe in the spirit of "This is Your Land;" that everyone should be able to enjoying our natural wonders.

The Lower Middle Economic 20%

Increased Work Hours and the Lower-Middle 20%

In 1999, families in this bracket worked an average of 2,200 hours a year, or forty-four hours a week. (15) From 1979-1999, real mean income dropped from $25,931 to $24,568, a loss of 5.3%. (16) During this same period the number of hours worked by women increased from 690 per year to 1,650, or 13% to 30% of total family earnings, the sharpest increase of any economic quintile. (17) However, according to the report *New Skills for the New Economy*, the work hours for women have likely reached their ceiling. (18)

How do we offset the increase in work hours for members of the second lowest earnings bracket? A time bank can help family members too old or disabled to hold a full time job can exchange services and make new friends through the social activities. Older family members might be able to stay independent longer. One of the best ways to build local health is to utilize the information on pedbikeinfo.org and the models on the Safe Routes website to build network of pathways. Chapter Three has many more ideas for the poor and struggling.

The Role of High School for the Lower Middle 20%

In 1999 only 13.3% of people in this quintile had a college degree (19), compared to 25.5% for members of all groups. This suggests that the lack of college degree prevents many in this group from making more money. For that reason, many high schools emphasize the importance of a college preparatory curriculum. While this is laudable, we need other steps.

What are areas to focus on to increase the value of education for members of this group? Sending more people to college is a good goal; another is to focus on maximizing a high school education in the five ways addressed in Chapter One. Greater utilization of vocational programs, teaching personal finance in math class, effective physical education, skills oriented language programs and the option of daily art class is a good start.

Opportunities at Universities for the Lower Middle Twenty Percent

Why are the points made in the Chapter One section on special education are also especially relevant here? Children from families with less money are more likely to wind up in special education programs. This book advocates stepping outside the box to look at every possible way to improve the quality of the school day. Two core aspects of this discussion should be how to serve the healthiest possible food and making walk-to-school programs happen. The group *Safe Routes* offers models for walk-to-school programs.

As we know, the numbers in Table 2.2 suggest that a college degree has become more necessary for people looking to make more money. At the same time, paying for university is a large burden for families in this group.

How can we make college more accessible for this group? We should focus on keeping the price of universities low, at least at public colleges. "In 2010-11, the average amount of aid for a full-time undergraduate student was about $12,455, including more than $6,500 in grants that don't have to be repaid." (20) This is good news for aid recipients, but at the same time we need to keep prices down, which means looking at keeping administrative costs down and rather invest in properly supporting adjunct professors.

Crime in the Neighborhoods of the Lower Middle Twenty Percent

I believe it's safe to say that the near quadrupling of crime from 1960 to 1990 (21) means that both property and violent crime are not just a problem of low income neighborhoods anymore. The fact is that many people are struggling these days and it shows. To counter crime this book emphasizes healthy local economies that means jobs for everyone.

How do we make neighborhoods safer? Through building a local economy that includes vibrant local farms, co-ops and a good infrastructure of walking and bike paths. One problem is the younger generation spends their time tuned in to media instead of investing in themselves. "According to a Kaiser Family Foundation study, children between the ages 8 and 18 spend 6.5 hours per day on television, electronic games, computers, music and other media." (22) How to help kids unplug and spend more time working and playing in their hometowns is explored in Chapter Four; "Building Healthy Economies."

For example, through a local time bank a carpenter might find a few hours a week to share his trade with a student that in return showed him how to use a new program or piece of technology. This might even prevent high school drop-outs, who are reputedly responsible for a significant percentage of crime. (23) One example I know of a time bank creating employment for young people is through the *Merrimack Valley Time Exchange* in Massachusetts.

Building Health for the Lower Middle 20%

The research tell us that stress and depression levels in America are high for every group, but that no one suffers as do the poor. But what can be said about the second lowest quintile? The rise in work hours for women in this group was the sharpest, and we also know that increased costs in college, housing and health care hit this group especially hard.

How important are local economy goals for this group? Very; all of the local economy goals outlined in Chapter Four can help fight stress and depression, including thriving local farms, an easily accessible network of walking and bike paths, time banks, co-ops and shared housing. Booming local farms can provide easily accessible healthy food, which is key to good health. Local farms can also provide jobs, especially if local convenience stores commit to stocking some of their produce.

A solid, safe network of walking and bike paths can provide those who work locally with a healthy option to get to work or school. This is especially important for those on low incomes because transportation costs make up a very large portion of household budgets.

Time banks provide the system for people to build symbiotic relationships and get services they need. The Rushey Green Time Bank is a good model for improving physical and mental health of members, whereas the *Merrimack Valley Time Exchange* in Massachusetts is a good example of how a time bank can be used to employ young people and prepare them for the working world. However, the a real, positive trump card for so many of us is a huge increase in the role of the *Veterans Conservation Corp.*, which employs returning veterans in conservation projects that are good for everyone. Imagine what moving even one billion dollars of defense spending to this program could do!

What role can community recreation play in reducing stress and depression? I believe that some of the models outlined in Chapter Four could make a big difference. In my experience, in summer rich people go to country clubs and the rest of us go to crowded public facilities. I only noticed this after a three year stay in Germany, (at which time I paid about three dollars) to go to the community pools that usually consisted of three fifty meter pools; one for diving, one for laps and one shallow pool for kids (and water slide!) There were also volleyball courts, a big grassy area and plenty of parking, all for five bucks.

I believe we can resolve part of this dichotomy between very expensive private clubs and overcrowded public facilities through the semi-public German model of summer fun. It could provide America's struggling middle class with more fun and relaxation; a nice reprieve from the many stresses they are under. See the section on "Summer Recreational Facilities" in Chapter Three for more about how this model might work for us.

Why is the Rushey Green Time Bank such a good model for fighting stress and depression and how does this interface with other local economy ideas? The doctor in charge of the group approached the health of those under his care from four angles.

First, he assured that everyone was contributing through their services. Second, members were getting much needed services in return. Third, people had fun through the group's activities. Fourth, people made friendships to share and reach health goals with those new friends made through the time bank. "Through joint projects between Rushey Green Time Bank and the *Rushey Green Group Practice*, time bank members can be actively involved in their own health care, and in the promotion of good health." (24)

Alone, these are four powerful steps, but become even more powerful when combined with a healthy local farming system. With thriving local farms people have access to fresh, healthy produce in stores near them, which means access to the food they need to be healthy.

The Middle Economic 20%

Increased Work Hours and the Middle Economic Twenty Percent

The middle twenty percent has also experienced a dramatic increase in work hours, with families working an average of 3,200 hours per year, or 64 hours a week. (25) The average income from 1979 to 1999 dropped from $39,179 to $38,797. (26) The average hourly wage was $16 an hour. 79.7% of income is received from wages, salaries and property income. (27) This group earned 15% of total income in 1999. (28) In my opinion, the two greatest needs of the middle class from this book are same as the needs of the two lower earning brackets; 1) Job creation and 2) Assuring the solvency of Social Security while keeping health care costs down to assure not too many precious dollars are not absorbed maintaining health.

How could time banking benefit this economic group? With families in this bracket already working 62 hours a week at $16 an hour (1999 numbers), one might think that the principal wage earners might be less interested in time banking for business purposes. However, time dollars could be spent on services that make life easier; such as help preparing for a big family party or organizing out of control paperwork. It should be remembered that many time bank services are those that don't exist in the marketplace. Older family members unable to hold a regular job but able to perform some work could stay connected through swapping services.

How big a deal is increased spending on the Veterans Conservation Corps. for this group? Veterans of all economic backgrounds could benefit greatly from this program. Part of the benefit of participation in the program is economic, but another part of it is emotional and spiritual; carrying out a conservation project that's good for everyone. This is especially true for veterans returning with serious injuries or emotional challenges; their work could be good for all kinds of different neighborhoods.

The Role of High School for the Middle Economic Twenty Percent

Most people in this bracket have a college education. (See Table 2.2) In other words, there is likely pressure to at least not make less than their parents did. What that means is that much of the focus in high school may be simply on getting into college.

Is a comprehensive high school the best option for middle-class towns? Many students may never even consider the option of vocational education, perhaps because the programs don't exist or maybe because they think college admissions might look down on this. Regardless, students should be able to consider doing a combination of traditional and vocational studies if that is the sort of training they need or want. One approach to make this happen can be through a "comprehensive high school," whereby both traditional and vocational schools co-exist under one roof.

More Necessary and Expensive Universities for the Middle 20%

Considering the numbers on the correlation between educational attainment and income, (see Table 2.2) it should come as no surprise that children of the middle class are often pressured to go to college. It seems that the best advice is simply a repeat of the best possible steps for everyone else; fight hard to keep the tuition down at high quality, affordable state universities.

Chapter Eight; Winning the Green Revolution on Campus There would be almost nothing better than the "disappearing" American middle class taking part in the very achievable goals of the Green Revolution; building up our network of walking and bike paths, supporting local farming or expanding our national park system while we still can. Most important is that students take part in problem-solving on campus in all the ways outlined in that chapter. That said, students can't do it alone; they need hundreds of new author to explore these themes as well as local papers to reestablish their importance.

Crime in the Neighborhoods for the Middle 20%

For families earning an average of $40,000 or more annually means there are more choices of places to live, but the quadrupling of crime between 1960 and 1990 means some crime has spilled into middle class neighborhoods. This is one reason the book focuses so much on vocational education; if there are enough slots for those who choose to learn a skill or trade (carpentry, plumbing or sheet metal) then he or she should be able to, which would assure *everyone* gets the skills they need to survive and not turn to crime.

Building Health for the Middle 20%

Any of the ideas in Chapter Seven; Building Health could be applied to the health and well-being of this and any other group. Ideally, each and every one of the ideas will be explored by new authors, local journalists and college classrooms in your area. (29)

The Upper Middle Economic 20%

Increased Work Hours It's with this quintile that the work hours among families become striking, with an average of 3,900 per year, or 78 hours per week. (30) This is an increase of about 7.2% from 1989. (See table 6.3) Average wages were $20 an hour for Massachusetts residents and $21 for U.S. residents. (31) This group earned 23.9% of total income. (32) They work an average of seventy-work hours per week per family in this group.

Table 2.4 Health Care Expenses, per capita 1970-2008 (33)

	1970	1980	1990	2000	2008
Monthly Expenditures	$30	$92	$235	$399	$640
Annual Expenditures	$356	$1,100	$2,814	$4,789	$7,681

Some might say that this is an "apples to apples" comparison as care has improved (by many definitions) a great deal between 1960 and the present. What the chart does clearly demonstrate is the increased financial burden families are feeling. Pointing out rising costs is easy; but what can we do about it? Coming up with a plan for getting costs down is the hard part.

The Role of High School for the Second Highest Twenty Percent

It stands to reason that many in this group may live in the wealthier upper middle class towns: ones with greater financial resources. Ideally they would effectively use that wealth to create greater opportunities in public education that can offset the fact that it's harder to build a life on a high school education alone. 27% of adults in this group have only a high school education, (see Table 2.2) so it stands to reason that there is considerable pressure for young people to go to college as well!

What is the core principle to follow to support? We've already said that towns should focus on assuring that there are enough seats for students in the different vocational disciplines. The difference is that these wealthier and upper middle class towns are more likely have the resources to make this happen. As someone from Massachusetts

The benefits of having enough seats for vocational education include; a) the option of a more balanced education, b) offering students the chance to acquire with marketable skills, c) allowing hands-on learners to be in the ideal learning environment and d) giving students that need it occupational therapy. This final point comes from seventeen years in education, including two years in Special Education, both of which taught me just how much good occupational therapy can do for young people.

Opportunities at Universities for the Second Highest Twenty Percent

Paying for increasingly necessary universities is also clearly a heavy burden for many in the second highest quintile. While they may have more resources, even one child choosing to attend private college instead of state college can offset extra earnings.

What is the point of the chart below? The only point to be made here is the importance of high quality public colleges, so parents at this income level have the option of not having their savings wiped out. This is even more striking now than in 1990.

Table 2.5 Tuition, Room and Board at 4 Year Colleges, 1990 vs. 2010 (34)

	1990	2010
Public in-state student	$5,330	$10,660
Private College	$15,025	$31,051

Crime in the Neighborhoods for the Second Highest Twenty Percent

Members of this quintile who live in neighborhoods have less reason to fear violent crime, but more reason to fear property crime. A study of New York City neighborhoods found "Some neighborhoods that tend to have lower real estate values and were among the five least safe neighborhoods for violent crimes — West Harlem (which includes Hamilton Heights and Sugar Hill) and East Harlem — were among the top five safest for property crimes, according to DNA info's Crime & Safety." (35) So, most of us are directly affected by crime, although obviously every neighborhood is affected somewhat differently.

How do the points on education relate to this situation? The five education points in this book can help, but teaching the basics of mortgage, finance, renting, credit and budgeting in school is one way to give young people the tools to survive, which will prevent them from resorting to crime

Building Health for the Second Highest Economic 20%

Comparing levels of stress and depression of different economic groups is hard. In fact, it's mere speculation. However, it's reasonable to assume that the large number of work hours is a factor. Based on personal experience, reading the research and observation, stress and anxiety can be handed down from parents to children.

What is the best book response? A good start is to have a look at the ideas in Chapter Three; Building Local Resources. I believe that the ideas there, if well implemented, have the power to have a true, positive impact on the lives of both parents and children. Walking and biking paths, time banks and co-ops are a few of the good things we can do.

How can we help older people with stress and depression? The Rushey Green Time Bank (36) is one of the original examples of a "fifty plus time bank," whose role is summed up in the words of their special edition newsletter. "Time Bank members can take part in a diverse range of activities, including health-orientated pursuits such as walking groups and chair-based exercise classes, as well as social events, film nights, arts and crafts, and days out, such as bowling and regular coffee-mornings." So, by now you should be able to see just how big a difference time banks can make!

The Highest Earning 20%

There is a great deal of variance of income within this group; some may have good jobs, although most are under considerable financial pressure to maintain their lifestyle.

Increased Work Hours for the Highest Earning 20%

The work hours for the highest earning twenty percent are amazing; families in this bracket work an average of 86 hours a week, more than two full time jobs. (37) According to the Massachusetts Institute for a New Commonwealth, "Married couples have been able to increase their incomes and standard of living largely due to the increased work effort of wives."

How large was the increase in work hours? From the period of 1979 to 1999 the average income of married couples increased 19.5%, during which time the average number of hours worked by wives increased from 13.4 per week to 32.1 hours per week nationally. (38)

How much did people in this group make per hour? Average hourly wages were thirty five dollars for Massachusetts residents, thirty-nine dollars for U.S. citizens. (39) This quintile earned 47.2% of total income in 1999, up from 43.3% in 1989. (40) This final fact confirms what most of us already know about the increasing concentration of wealth in the hands of a few.

How can we maintain quality of life for this group? One point is recognizing the value of having a friend to share and reach physical and mental health goals with. The original inspiration for this is the Rushey Green Time Bank.

One might think wealthier Americans might have little interest in time banking. After all, why would someone making fifty dollars an hour want to trade time with someone whose skill is only valued at eight dollars an hour by the market? People join time banks for different reasons. Someone with a good income can still benefit from the exchanges while other financially well-off people might find that supporting a time bank is a good way to give back.

The Role of High School for the Highest Economic 20%

It would be too easy to say we don't have to worry about education in the wealthiest quintile because people in it have more financial resources. After all, if they don't like their public schools they can afford private schools, right? Maybe yes, maybe no, but will certainly be expensive for all but the wealthiest of this group.

What is the role of vocational education and the top twenty percent? Although the urgency to acquire skills may be less for children from wealthier families, vocational education is for people of all backgrounds. As was explored in Chapter One, in Massachusetts only about seven percent of students utilize vocational education, although as many as thirty to forty percent would be better off in such programs, with as many as fifty percent doing a combination of the two. The hope is that they look down upon the trades; so, even though vocational schooling might be the best option for the student, snobbery can get in the way.

Why is it a bummer if members of this group reject vocational education? Good vocational programs can give hands-on learners growth and help acquiring marketable skills, which is good in any economy. Additionally, if wealthier communities lead the way with greater acceptance of vocational studies, perhaps other communities will follow through promoting more holistic, joy-filled school days for children in special education, as outlined in Chapter One.

Opportunities at Universities for the the Highest Economic 20%

Most parents in this economic bracket have attended college themselves (see Table 2.2) and may well expect their children to do the same. The good news is that families in this group can likely more easily pay for a state university, but those sending their children to private colleges will still be hard hit by the steep increase in college tuition over the past thirty years. $30,000 a year is still a steep price for all but the highest earners in this bracket, especially those with multiple children.

What is the best thing we can do in university education for this group? Explore the ideas in Chapter Eight on how our universities can make American colleges and universities places of problem solving. This is the right thing to do for rich or poor, although to keep it accessible to the poor we need to keep the tuition of state colleges affordable while exploring testing for credit options that can link those state colleges with town based learning.

Crime in the Neighborhoods for the Highest Twenty Percent

This quintile has less to worry about even the quadrupling of violent crime, but property crimes are absolutely an issue. Whereas wealthier members of society are arguably more sheltered from violent crime, property crimes are alive and well in neighborhoods of all income levels.

What is the best way to prevent property crime? I hope that people will not act out of fear and create draconian local codes. After all, as Yoda said; "Fear leads to hate and hate leads to the Dark Side." By contrast, I hope that more seek the joy that building a wonderful future for all of us can bring. A safe, healthy network of walking and bike paths is a good start. Large numbers of people in a town can use could make it safer, especially with proper lighting. Ideally, we can provide the infrastructure for a healthy lifestyle while reconnecting people walking and bike paths.

Building Health for the Highest Economic Twenty Percent

For this group the greatest threat may be the stress caused by the high number of work hours. At an average of eighty-six hours per week, this is more than two full-time jobs. The good news is that members of this group have more resources and can buy better food and health care.

Finally, what is some good news for analyzing the ideas in this chapter in a way that can benefit everyone? Good news for New Englanders is the decision of Fox 25 to employ twenty-five Northeastern journalism students to do investigative pieces. This model, if imitated by more colleges of journalism, could provide the manpower needed to breathe new life into investigative journalism, which is what is really needed to explore the ideas inside and outside the book the right way. So, props to Northeastern Professor Mike Beaudet for a model worth imitating, one can give us informed voices. Hope lives!

...

Chapter Two Questions

1. What did you think of the Mark Erlich quote at the beginning of the chapter?

2. How does the system of time banking work? How is it different from barter?

3. What is the single best step we can take for the poor?

4. What do you think are the best steps forward for the lowest economic 20%?

5. What economic group do you think the system of time banking can work best for? What do think is the potential of it to help the elderly?

6. Are there any assertions in the chapter that you do not agree with?

7. Do you think that time banking can help the elderly poor and/or struggling?

8. Did you learn anything from the health care chart?

9. What was the most interesting piece of information for you in the section on health care, housing and college education costs?

10. Do you agree with the Dwight D. Eisenhower quote?

3

Creating Opportunities for the Common Man

"Yes sir, my friends, the meek can only inherit the earth when the John Does start loving their neighbors. You'd better start right now. Don't wait till the game is called on account of darkness. Wake up, John Doe, you're the hope of the world."

-John Doe from the movie Meet John Doe

No one suffers like the poor. This is why this chapter presents ideas and principles with regard to housing, health, college costs and world peace that are designed specifically to help those that are struggling emotionally or financially. You will find good ideas in this chapter, but what's really needed is for others to expand upon them, which could easily be the source of sixty new books. That said, we need more than new authors to bring comfort to the suffering; we also need college classrooms that discuss these ideas and a new breed of journalists to analyze how they might positively affect members of their community.

Whereas the last chapter looked at ways for members of different economic groups to adapt to changing times, this chapter looks exclusively at ways for those that are struggling to find peace and joy. As with some later chapters I've chosen a question and answer format, as I believe that it will allow readers to more clearly see the ways we can help the most vulnerable.

Chapter Three Concerns

Q&A ON GREEN INFRASTRUCTURE FOR DEFENSE SPENDING

Q&A ON HOUSING FOR THE POOR AND STRUGGLING

Q&A ON HEALTH AND HEALTH CARE FOR THE POOR

. . .

Q&A on Green Infrastructure for Defense Spending

Why is it important to do cost-benefit analyses between warlike and peaceful solutions to situations? War always affects the most vulnerable the most, whether we're talking about death on the battlefield, famine or cuts to government services. For that reason we need to develop the capacity to undertake peace building projects so that when threatened with war we have clear choices. These informed choices will allow us to invest money into initiatives that can add to the well-being of communities, whether it is new walking and bike paths, solar installations or wells for clean water.

Table 3.1 Discretionary and Defense Spending in billions, 1990-2010 (1)

	1980	1990	2000	2010
Total Discretionary Spending	276	500	615	1,408
Defense Spending	135	300	295	714

Who should do these cost/benefit analyses? They can be done by college classrooms or local papers. Table 3.1 demonstrates just how much defense spending impacts federal spending. However, the game changer in the realm of transparency and investigative journalism happened when one Northeastern professor partnered with Fox 25 Boston for twenty-five of his students to do pieces for the T.V. station. *This* is what need; young people ready to do the analysis of federal spending that our overwhelmed media simply doesn't get to.

In the words of President Eisenhower; "Every gun that is made, every warship launched, every rocket fired signifies, in the final sense, a theft from those who hunger and are not fed, those who are cold and not clothed. This world in arms is not spending money alone. It is spending the sweat of its laborers, the genius of its scientists, and the hopes of its children." (2)

One of the most important aspects of making these analyses happen is through the further development of the capacity of local newspaper staff. However, I don't believe that local papers will develop this capacity organically; it will have to be the conscious choice of community members who say that; "yes, we want a paper that explores awesome projects for our community or national parks for our state." In my case, as a New

Englander, I'm desperately hoping that the Maine North Woods project goes forward, a project that would set aside about 3.2 million acres for wildlife habitat. The creation of this park would cost pennies compared to any defense spending and could be a great resource for everyone. Perhaps this goal of preserving such a huge chunk of the New England could be streamlined with the expansion of the Veteran's Conservation Corp., which employs returning veterans in conservation projects.

Quoting Eisenhower is easy; but what local infrastructure projects can we start with? We can start with a greater network of walking and bike paths, although for that we'll need "local experts," people with an intimate knowledge of their own city who have done the university coursework prescribed in the Pedestrian, Bike and Information Center (PBIC) handbook. Add that to the expansion and conservation of the national parks and we're really getting somewhere.

Local Experts and Safe Routes Programs

If planners want to spend $10,000 on walking and bike paths, we need people in the community who know how to use that money effectively. That is, someone who knows the planning, politics, budgeting and engineering involved in making walking and bike path projects happen. For this there are two main options; participating in *Safe Routes* programs or training people with the *Pedestrian, Bike and Information Center Compendium.*

How can we create these local experts, ones who understand all aspects of planning for achieving walking and bike paths? The PBIC Case Study Compendium is a good resource for colleges looking to offer coursework on the subject of building walking and bike paths. (3) It can serve as the basis of a syllabus of a college level course. Hopefully, soon we'll begin to see the growth of safe, viable walking options coordinated between private groups, local government and the U.S. Department of Transportation. The PBIC syllabus could be used as the basis of a course at a community or state college.

What colleges teach the coursework put together by the Pedestrian and Bike Information Center? Colleges that have coursework based upon the syllabus compiled by the PBIC include the University of California Berkeley, Portland State, University of Washington, Harvard School of Public Health, West Virginia, UCLA, Skidmore, Texas State, University of Illinois at Chicago, Augsburg College, Temple University, University of Oregon, Prescott College and the University of Bologna. (4) The significance of this is that for communities to effectively build their network of walking and bike paths they need to have people who have done this coursework. After learning about the complex environmental, political, budgeting and engineering dimensions of building walking paths, successful students can find ways to make these ideas a reality in their community.

The list of colleges above that offer these courses is as of July 2014; over time I hope that the list will grow. For those of us that live within New England, the Harvard School of Public Health seems to be the only option; perhaps in a few years every state will have one or two universities that offer the courses. (5)

What other roles can our universities play in building healthy, peaceful communities? As is explored in depth in Chapter Eight, they can lead the way as problem solvers and advocates of true good. Whether it's finding ways to support local farming, setting aside national parkland or building healthy local economies, the potential for college campuses to contribute is massive and largely untapped. Check out Chapter Eight to learn about those opportunities. Or, read how Fox 25 is utilizing Northeastern students as resources for producing true investigative journalism.

Q&A on Housing for the Poor and Struggling

Exactly how much have housing costs risen since 1978? From 1978 to 2010, the average price of a home rose from $120,000 to $375,000, putting the American dream of home ownership out of reach for many. (6) The chart below shows the average cost of a home and corresponding mortgage payment.

Table 3.2 Average Price of a Home, 1978 to 2010 (6)

	1980	1985	1995	2000	2005	2010
Average Home Cost	120,000	150,000	240,000	300,000	420,000	375,000
Average Monthly Payment	720	899	1,439	1,799	2,518	2,248

Note: The column monthly mortgage loan payment assumes a (ballpark) 6% interest rate for a thirty-year mortgage. You can use one of the many mortgage calculators on line for exact numbers.

Struggles of the Young to Find Housing

During four winters in New Hampshire I watched the prices of land go up and out of reach of many young people. Trailer parks were becoming a thing of the past, but with rising prices have again become the only option for many young couples.

I also remember my course in Adolescent Psychology in the spring of 2013. About half of the class was over thirty, but every single one of those under thirty was living at home with their parents, either in the basement or in their childhood room. The combination of higher rents and difficulty recent college graduates are having finding work is a part of this.

Are there any new housing models that can help the homeless? I believe co-ownership of real estate could work particularly well for the homeless, although lawyers need to write up very good co-ownership contracts that address all contingencies before this can work well. Without really good contracts, too many problems would present themselves. Also, many brokers I've spoken to have never even done a deal with multiple owners on the mortgage, so I don't know if they are prepared to deal with a homeless population looking to go in on housing together.

What is the role of local economies and affordable housing for the poor? A healthy local economy can provide the employment and support system for people to survive and get back on their feet. Co-ops, thriving local farms and especially the network of walking and bike paths discussed in Chapter Four are a good start toward creating this infrastructure. All of these opportunities are explored in depth in Chapter Four.

I remember a show about female veterans back from the war in Afghanistan, some of whom were looking to live in a group home. In short, women who had served their country and were struggling from post-traumatic stress disorder couldn't live in a group home because it violated zoning ordinances. This is where investigative journalism could really help; through research, writing and asking tough questions, they could help find solutions. This is one reason I find the decision of Fox 25 to use Northeastern students as writers is so significant; this new talent can support a new era of problem solving journalism. (7)

Again, if four or five homeless people could manage to overcome all the obstacles they face to make a shared ownership situation work, then it could be an example for others to follow. However, making this happen this will require both a great deal of work from lawyers designing good contracts, but also a healthy local economy that can provide enough employment for those making the (albeit small) mortgage payments.

What are some other examples of local economy jobs that could give homeless citizens work? I know that many companies in my home state of Massachusetts can't find enough skilled machinists; perhaps these are skills that could be acquired through training programs. With so many struggling with poverty and disease, I have to believe there are those that would jump at this opportunity.

Q&A on Health and Health Care for the Poor

Some aspects of health and health care are complicated, but some are not. The idea is to present the information here to help readers look at every possibility to build both good health and health care policies.

How much have health care costs gone up? In 1980 the average family about $92 a month for health care, but in 2008 that number had gone up to $640. Table 3.2 lets you see just how massive a jump that is.

Table 3.3 Health Care Costs, 1980-2008 (8)

	1980	1990	2000	2008
Average Annual Costs	$1,100	$2,814	$4,789	$7,681
Average Monthly Costs	$92	$235	$399	$640

What are the causes of the price increases in health care? *The New York Times* listed the following nine factors; increased use of sophisticated medical equipment, higher priced prescription drugs, arguably duplicative or unnecessary procedures, larger number of accidents that require medical attention, higher salaries for health care professionals and executives, malpractice insurance, administrative waste and fraud. (9) The next step for us is to see the percentages that each of these costs consist of.

One of the premises of this book is that college classrooms engage in analysis and problem solving in public policy. This is also true for health care; we need to increase our understanding of health care and the costs involved through doing constant comparison and analysis of the systems within each of the fifty states. This is one of the strengths of our federalist system and we need to take advantage of it through good college courses on the subject.

What book ideas are relevant to promoting good health for the poor? Chapter One offers some models for healthy school lunches, avoiding the pitfalls of "tracking" and the benefits of walk-to-school programs. The ideas in Chapter Four can play a role in building healthier communities. The ideas in Chapters Seven offer approaches to building wellness and Chapter Eight offers innovative ideas on how college campuses can lead us to a healthier lifestyle.

Dynamic Universities, Local Papers and Health

Our institutions of higher learning can do informed analysis as part of their course-work, work that is just too much for the media. Chapter Nine presents three examples of such college courses in New England. Just as adjunct professors need adequate support to teach well, local papers need solid support from the community to do their best work. The best example I am aware of this sort of symbiotic relationship between local papers and universities is the cooperation between Fox 25 Boston and a Northeastern University School of journalism class, whereby twenty-five journalism students will do investigate reports on social issues to be aired. In the words Fox News director Lee Rosenthal, "We look forward to making a difference by working with these students and Northeastern University." Make no mistake; this is a huge for New England as more pressing issues can be properly addressed. (9)

What role can good food play in our health? I defer to the quote of Hippocrates, who said; "Let thy food be thy medicine and thy medicine be thy food." How much of a difference would it make if we had access to big, juicy heirloom tomatoes, rather than those flavorless hockey pucks masquerading as tomatoes? Combine this with supporting local farms and building out network of walking and bike paths and we might even see an "epidemic of health."

What are the best movies I've seen on the subject of good food? I've found many good movies on Netflix that have taught me a lot about food and what it can do for our health. *Food Matters*, *Killer at Large* and *Forks Over Knives* all taught me the importance of food to cardiovascular health. *A Place at the Table* taught me about the different faces of childhood hunger.

How can we utilize the federalist system to improve our health care system? We have fifty states with fifty health systems to compare and learn from. These comparisons can help us see which systems work well, which need work and find those models worthy of adopting. One example model worthy of attention is the True North Clinic in Portland, Maine, where patients can use their "time dollars" to purchase health care services. (10) College level classes could look into what aspects of this model are worth imitating.

Building Opportunities for the Struggling in College

Rising college costs are putting enormous stresses on your average family. At a time when It is with this in mind that we look at some questions and answers that shed light on how we can best respond to the challenges of getting a good education without going deep into debt.

How much has the cost of college risen? According to an article in the Huffington Post, "college tuition and fees have increased 1,120 percent since records began in 1978....four times faster than the increase in the consumer price index." Example; Today, a typical New Hampshire family will spend around 60 percent of after-tax annual income on the $22,000 year tuition at UNH, up from 40% twenty-five years ago. This is before adding in food, shelter, health care and other costs. (11)

What is the best response to the rising cost of college? We should focus on keeping our state colleges affordable while promoting our local economies. The people need to express their need for affordable universities to their leaders, and then follow by utilizing the ideas in Chapter Four for building up opportunities, jobs and apprenticeships in their communities. Then young people will be able to continue to acquire useful knowledge that is affordable in an area where employment is not too difficult to find.

What is the most troubling statistic related to college? That 73% of recent college graduates still haven't found full-time employment. (12) The increase in the cost of paying for employee insurance is certainly one suspect for the decrease of hiring. So, studying ways to get health care costs down is also the study of increasing job creation. This is why we need local papers and universities to engage in analysis of health policy. This is also one reason why Northeastern Professor Beaudet's engaging twenty-five Northeastern students to do investigative journalism for Fox 25 Boston is exactly what we need. Props!

One response is to lower prices; a few private colleges are responding to the demand for lowering tuition costs as a tactic to attract new students. "Seton Hall University in South Orange, N.J., will offer the lowest tuition (roughly $10,000) for incoming freshmen with high grades" (13) Offering tuition this low is a strain; the key will be for colleges to keep infrastructure small.

What is the role of two year colleges? The advantages of two year colleges are that it takes less time to complete and costs less. For 2013-14, the average annual tuition for a two year college was a mere $2,960, especially interesting considering that most receive marketable skills from the experience. (14)

What is the role of teaching personal finance in high school to all of these issues? It's critical; people need to learn about how to manage money from a young age. When it comes to picking the right mortgage, health care package or college loans, people need to make smart decisions. The good news is that teaching young people about all this doesn't have to cost too much more money or take more time; instruction of this critical knowledge can be integrated into math class.

How do all of these ideas relate to assisting the struggling? Although each of the ideas can be strong alone, it is together that they have real power, which is the reason for putting them together in the table below.

Table 3.4 Ideas to be Explored for the Struggling

Education	Greater utilization of vocational programs, teaching personal finance, dynamic physical education, walk-to-school programs, healthy school lunches
Local Economies	Chapter Four explores approaches to healthy local economies, particularly important to those struggling. Healthy local farms means green jobs and food for health.
Securing Social Security	Chapter Five explores tactics to secure Social Security for the short and long-term, something that is utterly essential to the poor, especially the elderly poor.
Health and Well-being	Chapter Seven looks at approaches to building health and well-being, whereas Chapter Eight looks at "Winning the Green Revolution on College Campuses." Both chapter profile powerful ideas, people and organizations that can help.

As always, it's particularly important to involve three powerful entities in the process of exploring the above ideas; new authors, local newspapers and college classrooms. In this way I'm quite confident that thousands of authors, journalists, professors and students can make a tidy living and reap great satisfaction while contributing to the well-being of America's most needy.

. . .

Chapter Three Questions

1. What role can local farming play in the health of America's poor?

2. What do you think of the option of shared housing?

3. What is the importance of community members doing the coursework prescribed by the Pedestrian, Bike and Information Center?

4. Do you think flourishing local economies can could contribute to the development of young people?

5. How large a role do you think good food plays in our health? What changes need to happen for us to benefit even more?

6. Have you seen any good movies on the role of our food system to our health?

7. What is the relevance of the federalist system to our health care system?

8. What does the author believe is a good response to high tuitions?

9. What percentage of recent college graduates has no job?

10. Would you ever consider a two-year college for someone you know?

4

Building Healthy Economies

"Study and examine all but choose and follow the good."

-Ras Tafari

Now more than ever, we need strong and active communities that respond to our needs. With the onset of globalization and the financial crises, we need connections and partnerships at the local level. That is, people we trust and can work with. There are many steps forward we can take, which are the reason for the ideas here, all of which are applicable at the local level.

Chapter Four Concerns

A. CREATING WALKING AND BIKE TRAILS-Reflect on the role of the car in American communities. Then look at successful approaches to creating more walking and biking paths.

B.. TOWN BASED FUN-Tell how semi-public recreational facilities made for bright summer days in Europe. Then, imagine how that model can work in communities here.

C. BOSTON ARTS AND BUSINESS COUNCIL MODEL-Look at how shared housing can be a big plus for young, old and the communities they live in. Then reflect on a number of challenges with regards to this.

D. MAXIMIZING LIFE THROUGH EDUCATION-Look at how application of the main points in education can be a boost to communities, including making "every village a university" (1) through town based learning.

E. SUPPORT LOCAL FARMING-Not only do they support local economies and health, but can provide fresh fruit to local schools.

F. TIME BANKS AND THE LOCAL ECONOMY-Consider some ways that time banking can contribute to local life and be a part of healthy, local economies.

•••

The Current Suffering of Our Youth

Before going into some of the ways to help the younger generation, it's important to emphasize some of the ways that they're struggling. That is, some of the physical, emotional, economic and spiritual ways that younger people are having a tough time.

- Seventy-three percent of students one year out of college still have not found full-time employment, in contrast to forty-eight percent ten years ago.
- **A**lmost seventy percent of students take mood altering drugs.
- Twenty percent of children in America don't have food security.
- Anxiety and depression affect large numbers of young people. (1)

•••

Table 4.1 Summary of Chapter Points to Reverse the Malaise

Walking & Bike Trails	Build up our network of walking and bike paths through Safe Routes programs, rail trails and utilizing the information on the website pedbikeinfo.org.
Education	New authors, journalists, and college classrooms can explore all the aspects of Chapter One and Chapter Eight with an eye for how these ideas might be applied.
Healthy Local Economies	Young and old can benefit from the exploration of shared housing models, time banks,co-ops and healthy local farms.

Creating Walking and Bike Trails

It may seem strange to you to begin a discussion on local economies with talk about building walking and bike trails, but the fact is that a good network of these trails can contribute significantly to health and well-being, education, family fun and business. Like many others I used to believe that our dependence to the car was so great that we could never make these paths happen, but through the research I have learned that indeed we can.

How can good walking trails lead to better days at school? Walking to school can give children exercise, allow them to explore their world and feel more relaxed in their learning environment when they arrive at school. The national group *Safe Routes* has created walk-to-school programs in every state; you can read about their models on their interactive website, saferoutesinfo.org.

What is something else that readers should be aware of about Safe Routes? They produced an excellent video that tells the story of how the culture of walking to school has changed since 1960. The two minute video can easily get people up to speed on how children have been affected by the shift to a car-centric culture.

What is your own experience with these trails? After returning from three years in Europe, I found myself missing taking my bike everywhere; I missed the cozy, pedestrian-friendly European cities. However, in recent years I have had a great time exploring rail trails and bike paths on Boston's North Shore.

How do walking and bike trails promote health? With so many of our health problems related to diet and lifestyle, this should be a priority. Before we spend millions on parking garages, courthouses or road maintenance, we should also look at how that money can be used for building the infrastructure of walking and bike paths. That is, to do comprehensive cost/benefit analyses between the two.

What needs to happen to make these paths happen? More people need to do the coursework prescribed by the Pedestrian, Bike and Information Center. Before I read about some of the existing, successful models for building rail trails and bike paths on the pedbikeinfo.org site, I too thought it couldn't be done. Converting roads to biker or pedestrian use *will* require long-term planning but especially the creation of "local experts;" people with an intimate knowledge of both their community, planning, politics and budget issues. These experts will arise from relevant college coursework at area colleges, as prescribed by the Pedestrian Bike and Information Center handbook.

What colleges have offered the PBIC courses at their school? Colleges that have offered PBIC coursework for credit include University of California Berkeley, Portland State, University of Washington, Harvard School of Public Health, West Virginia, UCLA, Skidmore, Texas State, University of Illinois at Chicago, Augsburg College, Temple University, University of Oregon, Prescott College and the University of Bologna.

Past and Future of Railroads and Rail Trails

As we know, much of America grew up around the car, particularly in the suburbs and rural areas where people live much farther apart. Before the advent of the car one hundred years ago it was said that "one could start at any hour for almost any town in New England and make the journey in an incredibly short time" (2) Over the years those old tracks were gradually supplanted by cars, busses and motorcycles. North of Boston the Essex Railroad operated one single daily trip until 1959. (3) Since that time they lay untouched until the recent growth of "rail trails," which converted old railroad land into trails for walking, biking, jogging, and cross-country skiing.

Where do rail trails work best? Towns with land where railroads once ran now have a resource to convert to green space. These rail trails are win-win for towns because they use existing land and are often maintained by volunteers. Compared with pedestrian and bike lanes on streets that cost between $5,000 and $50,000 per mile, upgrading existing railroad land to "rail trails" is relatively affordable. That said, I still dream a big dream, of when walking and bike paths run along Route 95 in New England, from Providence to Bangor, Maine.

Pedestrian and Bike Paths

For ambitious town planners, here's a statistic; the cost of installing a bike lane is approximately "$3,100 to $31,000 per kilometer ($5,000 to $50,000 per mile), depending on the condition of the pavement, the need to remove and repaint the lane lines, the need to adjust signalization, and other factors. It is most cost efficient to create bicycle lanes during street reconstruction, street resurfacing, or at the time of original construction." (4) So, with costs reduced 90% if the path is built while the road is already under construction, it makes sense for towns to have committees aware of upcoming road work that they can then integrate walking and bike paths plans into the mix.

How can cities and towns work together on these projects? We need local experts that have done the coursework prescribed by the group Walking Info. Their syllabus prescribes coursework that can prepare students to be that point person in their community. For example, adding lanes during construction can reduce installation costs by about 90%, so it's worth the investment in the knowledge. However, I also believe that we have to be patient; it's logistically impossible to make this conversion overnight, but we could make it happen with a good fifteen to twenty year plan.

Safe Routes

The national organization Safe Routes has been very successful in helping to create safe walking routes for children to school. Apart from safety, they consider such factors as building a sense of neighborhood, fewer cars and emissions and giving children the exercise they need to focus in school. In short, local walking and bike enthusiasts should learn about and potential utilize their approach and success stories.

What kinds of communities have Safe Routes programs been successful in? Safe Routes programs have been successful in rural towns that have no options for children to walk to school. However, their programs have also been successful in cities. Some of these success stories are profiled in Chapter Eight, more can be found on the interactive map on their website.

How are these trails particularly relevant to progress in education for the struggling? To answer this question I have to be a bit subjective, but a good network of good trails is particularly relevant to students from low income families. As you may remember from reading Chapter One, adding quality walking and bike lanes to streets already under reconstruction is one approach to adding to the wellness of young people; the ideas outlined in the chart above are others. Adding bike lanes to a city's streets will not solve all the problems in education, but combined with better food and other education and local economy points it can make a difference.

Town Based Summer Fun

In many parts of New England there is a large dichotomy between expensive country clubs and the free, often overcrowded municipal pools. In my experience, there are few options in between. Some are lucky enough to live near lakes or oceans, but I believe we can add a new dimension to community life with the semi-public summer recreational model that added a lot to my life during my years in Europe.

What were the facilities like? Awesome; during the summers of 1995-1997 I was working in Europe for small wages, but I could afford to pay the three dollars to go to the fun summer recreation centers. The typical facility had two fifty meter pools; one for laps and one with a big shallow end for kids with a long slide, which was a blast. There was a diving pool, a big grassy area for sports, volleyball, plenty of parking and a beer garden. When I returned to the U.S., I dreamed of promoting the same model here.

Could this model work in the United States? With many towns strapped for money, it's a tough sell. However, advocates should consider the positive effect such facilities can have on property values, resisting development and community fun. People are feeling increasingly isolated and this is a chance to inject some real fun in people's lives.

How much space do you need? The average complex was about three to four acres in cities, and as much as seven to eight acres in rural areas. Finding the land to build these areas will be next to impossible in the city, but quite possible in rural areas. I know in my home region of New England there are lots of towns that this would be great for. This model is also profiled in the chapter "Building Health" because of the role it could play in reducing the isolation that so many feel.

Alone, the recreational facilities can add a lot to local life, but if combined with building our network of walking and bike paths, the positive impact on young and old could be huge.

Making Shared Home Ownership Viable

The idea of shared ownership appears in multiple chapters of this book, but it is of particular value helping people build capital and pay a small mortgage instead of high rent. I think of many groups with regards to this model; young people looking to build capital, older people looking to downsize, returning veterans with PTSD or individuals struggling to stay a float economically.

Why is this section called "Making Shared Home Ownership Viable" and not Shared Home Ownership? Because there is a great deal of work to be done before people can enter into these arrangements without too much risk. First and foremost, lawyers need to work on contracts that protect people.

How does shared housing relate to economic survival? Young people not earning much money can pay a small mortgage and build capital instead of high rent or having to live at home. A $1200 a month payment mortgage can buy a house most places these days, but imagine if that cost was split three ways. The owners could split costs as well as the work that goes into home ownership. Even three young people working for minimum wage should be able to afford partial ownership, although of course zoning and parking issues have to be considered. The point is that it can help give young people hope and a future!

This sounds good, but what if someone tries to get out of the deal? You need to have a really good contract that has clauses for every contingency. Again, this is something for lawyers to work on.

Do you know anyone that actually bought a home together? Yes. After graduating from Boston College in 1993, four classmates bought an apartment together. Alone, none of them made enough money to buy a place, but together they were able pay the down payment and mortgage for an apartment in Brookline, Mass. As each of them got married and moved out, they sold their share to those remaining. It was win-win; they didn't waste money on rent, and had the capital for a home of their own when they were ready.

Why doesn't this sort of thing exist now? As you know it was Boston College alums who participated in this successful experiment in communal finances, but today I think not enough young people know this option exists. But— and this is key — schools need to teach this knowledge of real-world money management principles in order for young people to have a chance to make this happen. This is especially true with high school students from families of modest means that don't acquire this knowledge in the home.

Can you think of any particular groups shared ownership would be useful for? It could be a great blessing for returning veterans or older people looking to downsize. I used to think about the potential a great deal when I was working with struggling students at a high school in northeastern Massachusetts. For many, the only options were low-paying labor or jobs in fast food restaurants. After taxes, many of them might earn $15,000 a year— an amount with which it's almost impossible to buy a home, which creates desperation in many. But if more high school and/or college graduates were able to "go in" together on a property, they too might enjoy the experience that my Boston College friends had; building capital while paying a low mortgage instead of high rent.

What are other aspects of making shared ownership work? First and foremost, the students need to have a solid understanding of mortgages, budgeting and credit. Second, people need to find towns where zoning allows for such arrangements. Third, real estate brokers need to provide information on how customers can have a contract that protects everyone in every contingency. This third and final point is perhaps the most important; there is a great deal of hard work to be done one constructing solid contracts that address every contingency before this becomes a truly viable option.

Table 4.3 Payments for a $300,000 mortgage (5)

	1 Payer	2 Payers	3 Payers	4 Payers	5 Payers
Monthly Payment	$1800	$900	$600	$450	$360

Note: The numbers above are a rough estimate of costs associated with ownership, including mortgage payments, taxes and insurance. This does not include maintenance as it is but a rough chart for others to further develop.

How is partial home ownership good for local business? Even a small percentage of townspeople paying a smaller mortgage can free up money to be spent on local businesses, rather than sent in monthly payments to Wall St. banks. Finding ways to keep money local should be a priority.

Can shared ownership be good for safety? I believe that the presence of even a few co-owned houses on any block can make that area safer. Consider the attitude difference between five young people struggling to pay rent with those same five young paying a small mortgage and building capital. Clearly the partial owners of a property are going to be much more invested in the neighborhood and businesses in the area.

Can shared ownership help with homelessness? I think so, but only if lots of lawyers work hard to come up with good contracts to protect people from risk. Since the onset of the mortgage crisis in August of 2007, homelessness has hit hard and leaders should have a look at different models of co-ownership. Simply put, three or four adults with full-time, minimum wage jobs should be able to afford a house. Challenges include zoning, a good contract and building trust between co-owners. Clearly making this working is going to require a lot of people to work together.

Aspects of a Co-ownership Contract

Of course prospective owners always need to protect themselves and their investment. One (Australian) real estate agency's version of a co-ownership contract spoke to the need for having clauses that address every possible contingency. Some contingencies that group stated should be addressed in a contract include; someone backing out, operating expenses, obligations of co-owners to pay their share on time, ways of selling out, either collectively or individually; a way of dividing up any profits or losses, an approval mechanism for allowing people other than the owners to live at the property and a regime to protect a co-owner against default.

What exactly has to happen for this to work for struggling youth and older people looking to downsize? A whole lot of people have to work together on this project for it to work, from educators to lawyers to city leaders community and family members. The role of educators is to teach the basics of mortgage, financing, renting and credit in the schools, ideally as part of math class. Lawyers in real estate offices need to work on really good contracts and all of us need to work on building healthy local economies that help us build quality relationships, ones that we need for effective collaboration.

Boston Arts and Business Council Model

As working adults, our needs for fun, excitement or involvement are not always being met. Some of us might like to get involved in the local arts or music scene, but how do we go about doing that? The *Boston Arts and Business Council* exists to get artists and professionals together in mutually beneficial relationships, which is a model that could be repeated in more cities.

How does the BABC connect artists with professionals? Large, established arts groups may have enough support, but smaller, local arts organizations often struggle to survive. The BABC matches professionals with a love for the arts with an arts organization that needs support, be it legal, artistic or business oriented. A small theater group might get money advice from a financial consultant or free legal advice from a lawyer. In return, the professional gets to be part of an arts organization.

Does the council offer training for future board members? The Council not only helps find permanent board members for the organizations, but they run courses designed to train future board members or trustees. (7) In short, it's a win-win organization for any community; arts organizations get the support they need and those who give their time and money get to put some art and creativity in their life.

Could the BABC model be expanded to other roles? Sure, one example would be for future politicians; coursework could be created that prepared city council members or state reps for service. Completion of such coursework might make candidates more competitive and clear the way for constructive debate during campaigns that could benefit the people.

Maximizing Life through education

Some say that every child needs a village and others say that every village needs children, but clearly both are true. Simply put, not only is it harder to build a life on a high school education than it was twenty years ago, (8) but even recent college graduates are having a hard time finding work. In fact, as of 2011, seventy-three percent of students one year out of college still had not found full-time work. So, it only makes sense to focus on ways that communities can help residents build quality of life through education. For that reason the following points in education are reviewed.

Eight Steps Forward in Education

First, we should assure that students that want to learn a trade able to do so, that there are enough slots for students that are serious about acquiring a trade. It's very important that students use the time in high school well, either getting a solid classical education, acquiring a useful skill or both. Offering the option of doing a *combination* of vocational and traditional studies is one way to bring young people into the modern world.

Second, the existing, successful examples of walk-to-school programs of the national group *Safe Routes* should be studied at our public state colleges.

Third, students should have the option of daily physical education to learn how to maintain and improve their health and well-being through physical activity.

Fourth, students should learn the fundamentals of mortgage, finance, budgeting, renting and credit, ideally integrating the instruction of these topics into math class.

Fifth, adult education, certification or testing for credit programs could be integrated with state colleges that offer exams for credit. Thoreau was right when he said that "every village should become a university." Ten years ago this idea might not have gained wide acceptance, but today we need good ideas!

Sixth, we should concentrate on making school lunches as healthy as possible, utilizing models from the British chef Jamie Oliver or the French movie *Les Enfants Nous Accuseront.*

Seventh, daily art should be an option for all students; this can allow for great emotional growth and skill acquisition.

Eighth, the practice of "tracking" should be looked at, whereby the learning capacity of students is judged globally from a young age. The tendency is to put struggling students alone with work sheets, whereas what students need is the opposite; rich content, group problem solving and other activities with peers. One excellent article on the subject is one by a Dr. Shankers. (see Bibliography)

In the 19th century Henry David Thoreau wrote that "it's time to make villages universities" and "that there is no reason for 19th century life to be provincial." (9) Not much has changed; there are many who dream of learning being a life-long process. Ideally, our state and community college system can use "testing for credit" options to spice up local learning.

The Core Principle

We need a college system that recognizes knowledge for its own sake. So, if you could demonstrate knowledge in a subject area and prove it on a test, then you should get credit for it, right? There would be no need for people to travel so far or pay so much. Residents could work in classrooms with people from their own area. All they would have to do is to find someone to teach the course.

Should there be requirements for where courses are done? Perhaps the university could insist that at least half of the courses be done on campus, for example. The good news is that educators and lawmakers don't have to see this as a threat; the system could feed back into local and state colleges if it was done right. I say this from the perspective of someone who teaches languages but also enjoys studying them.

Support Local Farming

A strong system of small farms provides a very good base for both the local economy and local health. Many local farms are struggling to survive, just as many struggle with their health. We need symbiotic relationships with good communication between local farms and people that will build healthy lives.

There are four main ways to support local, healthy food; each of them provides multi-faceted benefits to everyone involved.

Community Supported Agriculture

When people buy shares of "CSAs" or community supported agriculture they pay a flat price to the farmer for a weekly share of the harvest. Customers get a good, healthy food every week while reducing risk for the farmer because he gets paid in advance.

Farmer's Markets

Going to hometown farmer's markets gives us access to healthy, local produce while reconnecting farmers with customers. We can get to know the farmers and they can get to know us. This is also a good for restaurants; it can be fun for consumers to see the name of the farm that produced the food when they know the farmer. This was a point made clear in the movie *Food Matters*.

Schools

Committing to serving food produced at local farms in the schools is the best step forward we can take for to revive our health and local agriculture. This is also true for colleges; can you imagine the impact on the local economy of a college of 10,000 that committed to buying from local farms? It would be huge. One good French movie that looked at the effect of serving locally grown food in the schools was *Les Enfants Nous Accuseront*. An English chef to learn from is Jamie Oliver. In my home state of Massachusetts, the Farm to Table program out of Amherst, Massachusetts is one example of a good program to bring locally grown food into the schools.

Fresh Food Section

I wish that more of us could buy quality fruits and vegetables from convenience stores. Like many people, I have to go a few miles to a supermarket to get fresh food, while the small stores seem to have few quality options for fresh produce. When they do have tomatoes, they tend to be like flavorless hockey pucks. I want to see delicious, locally grown tomatoes at the little stores near me. This is especially important for older people that have a hard time getting around; they need easy access to the food that will allow them to build their health.

TIME BANKS AND THE LOCAL ECONOMY

Time banks are a new version of an old idea; one of neighbor helping neighbor. As one of the founders of the group Hour World said; "time banks are one spoke in the wheel of the local economy." They can help create symbiotic relationships and the structure to assure that *everyone* has a role in the economy, from young people from underemployed neighborhoods to older, isolated residents.

Who came up with the idea of time banking? Reborn in Edgar Cahn's book "Time Dollars," (10) this simple idea can have a powerful effect on American communities. It is similar to barter in that one person is helping another without a cash payment, but there is a third component.

How does the system work? If a time bank member does an hour of work for another member, he can get his hour of service back from any other member, not just the person he performs the service for. In fact, most take their services back from someone other than the person they helped. This way, there is variety in the services that members can spend the "time dollars" on.

Neighbors Helping Neighbor

We already know that in the time banking system, people do what they enjoy for others while receiving services in return. This means that neighbors are working together and getting to know each other in a good way; through working together.

What's a good way to insure member success? Members are encouraged to offer services that they truly enjoy. After all, when you get a call for a service, you want to be glad that you got it. For example, if an accountant who works forty hours a week enjoys raking leaves, then she should offer that as a service. The goal is for everyone to stay active doing what they love.

How do time banks create to communities? For people that are feeling isolated, time banks offer a communal aspect that's too often missing. Monthly potluck suppers are one event that can help people get to know each other. Generally, events are fun and relaxed because everyone is just looking to share time doing what they enjoy. What's important is that people are connecting in productive ways that don't always happen within a money-based economy.

Time Banking for Older People

The three main benefits of time banks to older people are; giving and receiving services, making friends and finding people to share and reach health goals with.

How do time banks integrate older people into the economy? Some are too old or sick to hold a regular job, but they might still be capable of doing things that are valuable to someone else. For example, they might be able to sew, watch a pet or teach someone young how to read. How many older people are sitting at home alone when they could be contributing in this way? Quite a few I'm sure, which is one reason I am so motivated to see more time banks provide this structure for older people.

How can they help older people reach health goals? Time banks can help otherwise isolated people make symbiotic friendships, as demonstrated by a case study example of the *Rushey Green Time Bank* in England. Founded to help offset the isolation that can plague hospital patients, researchers found that building the connections between group members was of key importance to building health. (11) Not only were the friendships in and of themselves important to the well-being of patients, but some used those friendships to share and reach health goals together. Clearly this is a model that bears imitation!

Young People and Time Banking

This system has great potential for disenfranchised youth. Generally young people want jobs that pay money, not time dollars, but time banks can help students acquire skills and knowledge for school or get services that can help them. However, as of March 2015 I was only aware of one time bank that catered to young people; the Merrimack Valley Time bank in Lowell, Ma; part of the *Coalition for a Better Acre.*

What is one good argument for time banks for young people? Contrast this with the existing culture, whereby "Young people today spend an average of almost 6.5 hours a day with media." (12) Some may think they don't have a skill to share, but a tech-savvy high school student might show a carpenter how to use some new computer software, and in return be shown a bit of carpentry. Involvement in the right time bank can give young people opportunities they otherwise wouldn't have.

What is my dream use of time banks for older Americans? I would love to see older people take time to talk with each other about how to use their Social Security benefits. Remember; time banks offer services that don't exist in the market economy; one example could be a member talking with another member about how she uses her Social Security or Medicaid benefits to build her health.

Table 4. 4 **Chapter Four Themes of Building Healthy Communities**

Supporting Local Farms	Healthy local farms help give people access to the food they need to feel their best. Farms are also a source of labor, seasonal work for students and green space.
Walking and Bike Paths	A dynamic network of walking and bike paths, rail trails, and Safe Routes programs can boost healthy options. Ideal is to have community members with PBIC training; see the website pedbikeinfo.org for more info.
Chapter Seven Themes	Chapter Seven looks at many more health themes to be asked and answered together, ideally through new books, journalists at local papers and college classrooms.

•••

Chapter Four Questions

1. Are there any rail trails or land for rail trails near you?
2. Do you think there would be support in your community for the Safe Routes walk to school programs?
3. According to the text, how much does it cost to build new pedestrian or bike paths?
4. What is the more affordable alternative to building new bike and walking paths?
5. What did you think of the summer recreational facilities model?
6. Do you think the Boston Arts and Business Council model could work near you?
7. What subjects in this chapter that could be explored as full books?
8. Do you know anyone that the co-ownership model could work for?
9. Can you think of anyone older that the time bank model would benefit? Could it be altered to work for high school or college students?
10. How would you improve upon the graph at the end of the chapter?

5
Securing and Maximizing Social Security

"All of us who are concerned for peace and triumph of reason and justice must be keenly aware how small an influence reason and honest good will exert upon events in the political field."

-Albert Einstein

Simply put, federal policies are threatening the stability of our country. If the younger generation is going to enjoy the quality of life so many older people have through this program, then we need to 1) Get federal spending under control and 2) Work together to find ways to maximize our Social Security checks, which in large part means keeping health care costs down. This chapter is not designed as a comprehensive study guide for the federal budget, but it will provide you with is some tables and perspectives for better understanding our federal budget and how to keep it solvent enough for Social Security to function at *one hundred percent capacity*. I believe that Social Security may be the best program we have and working together on this is ripe with positive potential.

The quote from Einstein is at the beginning of this chapter to remind readers how important it is that more hard-working Americans understand our federal policy choices, as opposed to leaving all the work to the politicians.

Chapter Five Concerns

*** If you are only interested in steps to secure and maximize Social Security, then you can skip ahead to Section D. For those interested in some perspectives on federal spending as a whole should read the rest.**

A. FEDERAL SPENDING FROM 1776 TO 2000 -Show the chronology and growth of federal revenue, spending, deficits and debt from 1776 until 2000. What follows are tables of Post War deficit spending, followed by perspectives on spending and revenue for the 1946-2000 period.

B. CURRENT FEDERAL REVENUE AND SPENDING-Readers can view core information on how the federal government spends our money, by category and department. We then look at the state of Social Security, followed by ways for making that system and federal spending work better for people.

C. ENTER THE BIG DEFICITS 2000-2020- Look at spending and revenue trends for the first two decades of the 21st century. A time of great change, we also look at trends, projections and the need for greater cooperation between the media and universities in doing good analysis.

D. SECURING AND MAXIMIZING SOCIAL SECURITY-A look at two ways to make the system work for current and future generations. Then, we consider the kind of cooperation required by the media and universities for creating a good, long-term plan that will secure the retirement of our children and grandchildren.

E. AVENUES TO PROGRESS-Look at some good work of authors, economists, professors and organizations on the subject of sane long-term approaches to federal spending. We also look at the potential of college classrooms, the media and such programs as the *Veterans Conservation Corps.* to contribute to.

. . .

FEDERAL SPENDING FROM 1776 TO 2000

As my old landscaping boss Louis used to say; "if you don't know where you're coming from you don't know where you're going to." In the case of the federal government, it's good to see some changes that have occurred over the years.

Until the Second World War our budget remained relatively well balanced, with only a few years of deficit spending. For our first 60 years as a nation (through 1849) budget surpluses and deficits yielded a net surplus of $70 million. The Civil War, along with the Spanish-American War and the depression of the 1890's, resulted in a total debt of just under $1 billion in the 1850-1900 period. Between 1900 and 1916, the budget was always close to balanced.

When was the next period of deficit spending? The combination of the Great Depression followed by World War Two resulted in a long run of deficit spending. As a result, federal debt erupted from less than $3 billion in 1917 to $16 billion in 1930 and then to $242 billion by 1946. In relation to the size of the economy, debt held by the public grew from 16 percent of GDP in 1930 to 109 percent in 1946. The chart below should help. (2)

Table 5.1 Budget Statistics, 1776 until World War Two (in millions)

	Receipts	Outlays	Surplus or Deficit
1789-1849	1,160	1,090	+70
1850-1900	14,462	15,453	-991
1920	6,649	6,358	+291
1930	4,058	3,320	+738
1940	6,548	9,468	-2,920
1946	39,296	55,232	-15,936

When were our first significant deficits as a nation? World War 1 brought large deficits that totaled $23 billion over the 1917-1919 period. The budget was then in surplus throughout the 1920's.

When did post World War One spending taper off? In 1920 the government ran a surplus, although in 1919 the government spent almost four times what it took in as a result of the tail end of World War One. This sort of deficit spending was not matched again until 1943, with receipts of $24,001 million to outlays of $78,555 million. (3)

When was the federal income tax introduced? Prior to 1913, income taxes did not exist or were minimal, other than for a brief time during the Civil War period, when special tax legislation raised the income tax share of federal receipts during the following decade. By 1930, the Federal Government was relying on income taxes for 60 percent of income.

What are the top current sources of revenue? As of 2010, much of government is funded through individual income taxes, Social Security or other payroll taxes. Estimated income for fiscal year 2010 were $2.165 trillion, an estimated decrease of 11% from 2009. (4) Revenue came from individual income taxes, Social Security and corporate income taxes.

Post World War Two Deficits

During much of the post-World War Two period, large deficits were incurred only in wartime (Korea and Vietnam) or as a result of recessions. Before the 1980's, postwar deficits as a percent of GDP reached their highest during the 1975-76 recession at 4.2 percent in 1976. (5) Debt held by the public had grown to $477 billion by 1976, but, because the economy had grown faster, debt as a percent of GDP had declined throughout the postwar period to a low of 23.9 percent in 1974, and went back up to 27.5 percent in 1976. (6)

Table 5.2 Revenue, Spending and Deficits, 1946-2000 (billions) (7)

	Revenue	Spending	Surplus or Deficit
1946	$39.296	$55.2	-15.9
1960	$92.5	$92.1	+301
1980	$517.1	$590.9	-73.8
1990	$1,032	$1,253	-221.0
2000	$2,025	$1,788	+236.2

When did the habit of deficit spending begin? Until 1980 the federal government didn't record large deficits outside of wartime, but by the 1990's it was an established precedent. Both the Bush Sr. and Clinton years saw relative discipline, although Congress sharply increased spending during the 1990's.

Why does deficits as a percentage of GDP matter? It's one reflection of our indebtedness. After five years of deficits averaging only 2.5 percent of Gross Domestic Product between 1977 and 1981, debt held by the public stood at 25.8 percent of GDP by 1981. (8)

Have we managed to achieve a surplus in modern times? Yes. As you can see in Table 5.9, revenue nearly doubled from 1990-2000, which allowed for greater spending and a surplus, which is historically unprecedented. Who gets to spend double and have a surplus? No other Congress in recent years has had that luxury.

How does the surplus spending of 2000 compare with 2014? In the year 2000 the surplus peaked at $236 billion, an amazing accomplishment by today's standards. However, it should be noted a near doubling in revenue between 1990 and 2000 (from one to two trillion) enabled the "surplus years". (9)

CURRENT FEDERAL REVENUE & SPENDING

During fiscal year 2012 the federal government collected approximately $2.45 trillion in tax revenue, up $147 billion from 2011 revenues of $2.30 trillion. The three primary sources of revenue are income taxes, Social Security and corporate taxes.

Table 5.3 Federal Revenue, 2012 (10)

Category	Total Revenue	Percent of Total
Income Taxes	$1,132 Billion	47%
Social Security	$845 Billion	35%
Corporate Taxes	$242 Billion	10%
Other Revenue	$216 Billion	8%

Notes on Federal Revenue A good economy can mean a big increase in revenue. One example is 2000-2001, during which time revenue leaped from one to two billion. The unique nature of Social Security revenue means that Social Security payroll taxes go to the Social Security trust fund, which is only for Social Security payouts. Like income taxes, corporate taxes are also affected fluctuations due to the economy.

Table 5.4 Top Federal Spending Categories, 2012

Category	2012 Spending	% of Total
Defense	$670 Billion	19%
Social Security	$1.3 Trillion	37%
Medicare & Medicaid	$802 billion	23%
Interest	$461 billion	13%

What are other examples of the effect of the economy on revenues? Typically, recessions mean lower tax collections as economic activity slows. For example, tax revenues declined from $2.5 trillion in 2008 to $2.1 trillion in 2009, and remained at that level in 2010. From 2008 to 2009, individual income taxes declined 20%, while corporate taxes declined 50%. (11)

A common measure of the level of taxation or government spending is the size of that spending compared to Gross Domestic product. Tax revenues averaged approximately 18.3% of gross domestic product (GDP) over the 1970-2009 period, generally ranging plus or minus 2% from that level. When looking at the level of government involvement in the economies of other nations, this is one indicator. At 15.1% of GDP, the 2009 and 2010 collections were the lowest level of the past 50 years. 2012 spending made up 22.8% of GDP, versus 2011 spending 24.1% of GDP. (12)

What is current federal spending? During Fiscal Year 2012 the federal government spent $3.54 trillion, down $60 billion or 7% from Fiscal Year 2011 spending of $3.60 trillion. The top five spending categories are Defense, Social Security, Medicare, Medicaid and interest on the debt. My two main personal interests with regard to federal spending are; 1) A focus on securing Social Security long-term and 2) Moving defense spending to the Veterans Conservation Corp. to support positive veteran employment.

How much has defense spending increased and what is the effect of this? It has increased massively over the years and in my opinion is what we need to look at to get our long-term debt under control.

What is Social Security? Social Security is a federal social insurance program that provides income for retirees and the disabled. Created in 1937, the system is designed to help people with their retirement. Another perspective is that it was designed to help the elderly poor.

The Functions and Costs of Medicare

Combined Medicare and Medicaid spending made up 23% of federal spending in 2012. Medicare is an insurance program whereas Medicaid is an assistance program that serves low-income people of all ages. Medical bills are paid from trust funds which those covered have paid into. It primarily serves people over 65, whatever their income. It also serves younger, disabled people and dialysis patients. Patients pay part of costs through deductibles for hospital and other costs. Small monthly premiums are required for non-hospital coverage.

Who runs Medicare and how does the money flow? Medicare is a federal program, although it's run by the states. It is basically the same everywhere in the United States and is run by the Centers for Medicare & Medicaid Services, a federal agency.

What idea in the book is relevant to discussions of Medicare policy? Any steps that result in people acquiring the tools to systematically build their health and well-being are relevant. Access to healthy food and the steps to support vibrant local farms outlined in Chapter Three can play a huge role. That said, of any principle in health care policy, the most important might be to do in depth comparisons between the health care delivery systems of the fifty states. This use of the federalist system, as outlined in the U.S. constitution, may be the best tool we have.

The Functions and Costs of Medicaid

What is Medicaid? It is an assistance program that serves low-income people of all ages. Medical bills are paid from federal, state and local tax funds. Patients usually pay no part of costs for covered medical expenses, although a small co-payment is sometimes required. Medicaid is a federal-state program. It varies by state and is run by state and local governments within federal guidelines.

What aspect of public policy could positively affect people on Medicaid? Access to healthy, locally grown food could allow people on low incomes to let "food be thy medicine," as this book promotes. Four steps to building healthier local farms that will make healthy food accessible include; farmer's markets, community supported agriculture and more healthy produce in convenience stores. However, there is no substitute for universities to become active in analyzing the supporting long-term plans for making Medicaid and Social Security viable.

Mandatory vs. Discretionary Spending

The difference between mandatory and discretionary spending is important to understand. Federal spending is classified either as mandatory, with payments required by specific laws, or discretionary, with payment amounts renewed annually as part of the budget process. Mandatory spending includes Social Security, Medicare and required interest spending. Defense is the largest discretionary category, making up almost half of spending.

How did the nature of discretionary spending change from 1980 to 2010? Discretionary spending accounted for 34.0% of total federal spending in 2011, led by defense. In 2011 the top five discretionary spending categories were Defense, Health and Human Services, Transportation, Veteran's Affairs and International Programs.

Table 5.5 Discretionary Spending; The Big Three, 2011

Department of Defense (including overseas Contingency Operations)	$663.7 billion
Department of Health and Human Services	$78.7 billion
Department of Transportation	$72.5 billion

Table 5.6 Discretionary Spending, Numbers 4-8

Department of Veterans Affairs	$52.5 billion
International Programs	$51.7 billion
Urban Development	$47.5 billion
Department of State and other Department of Housing	$46.7 billion
Department of Homeland Security	$42.7 billion

How has mandatory versus discretionary spending changed? Over the past 40 years, the percent of "mandatory spending" for programs such as Medicare and Social Security has grown, while other "discretionary" categories have declined. The idea is that there were a few small items that absolutely couldn't be cut, although the programs that fall into that category now are huge. Between 1966 and 2006, Medicare and Social Security grew from 16% of the budget to 40%. (13) When spending is mostly mandatory it means that there is little opportunity for taxpayers to influence how their money is spent. Most discretionary budget spending now goes to defense, but $615 B or 17% of the total budget goes elsewhere. See Table 5.2. So, whereas the spending above is discretionary, or voted upon every year, the chart below shows the mandatory spending.

Table 5.7 Mandatory Spending, The Big Three in 2012

Total	$2.184 trillion
Social Security	$677.95 billion
Medicare	$453 billion
Medicaid	$290 billion

Table 5.8 Mandatory Spending, Categories 4-6

Interest	$164 billion
Other Mandatory Programs	$571 billion
Interest on Debt	$11 billion

What has caused Medicare costs to grow from sixteen to forty percent? I suspect that the increases in costs are related to increases in the price of health care. So, if we control health care costs then Medicare recipients get more for their money. However, for that we will more effective analysis of maximizing health care spending by the media and universities. That would require a great deal of cooperation, although a partnership between Northeastern University and Fox25 provides a model for this kind of communication. See the end of the chapter for more.

Defense and Homeland Security

The President's 2010 budget proposal for defense was $663.8 billion, including $533.8 billion for the Defense Department and $130 billion for work overseas, primarily the wars in Iraq and Afghanistan. This is a big jump from 2005, at which time defense spending was $494 billion. (14) As the chart below demonstrates, the percentage of discretionary spending that goes to defense hasn't changed much, but overall spending has.

Table 5.9 Defense & Total Discretionary Spending, 1970-2010 (15)

	1970	1980	1990	2000	2005	2010
Total Discretionary	120	276	500	614	968	1,408
Defense	82	135	300	295	494	714

What are some areas we can convert military spending into? I often dream of converting military spending into investment into our green infrastructure; biking and walking paths, rail trails and green education at our state colleges and universities. This may be possible in the future, but before that can happen we need to have "local experts," people that have done coursework prescribed by the Pedestrian Bike and Information Center. Once a community has someone with this training, they will be able to find all sorts of ways to convert federal money into walking and bike path infrastructure. You can read more about this in Chapter Three or go straight to the source of this information at the website pedbikeinfo.org

5.10 Top Discretionary Outlays for 2010

Department of Defense (including overseas Contingency Operations)	$663.7 billion
Department of Health and Human Services	$78.7 billion
Department of Transportation	$72.5 billion
Department of Veterans Affairs	$52.5 billion
International Programs	$51.7 billion
Urban Development	$47.5 billion
Department of State and other Department of Housing	$46.7 billion
Department of Homeland Security	$42.7 billion
Department of Education	$26.3 billion
Department of Energy	$26.0 billion

ENTER THE BIG DEFICITS 2000-2020

As of 2000, things were looking up; Congress had managed to agree on spending that produced surpluses in the years 1998-2001. However, it should be noted that this was no great feat of fiscal discipline; revenue had doubled from one to two trillion dollars in those years. So, the government had succeeded in not pissing away the sweat, tears and hard earned tax money of the American people for a few years, but that would not last.

The slow economy, large tax reductions and additional spending in response to the September 11, 2001 attacks produced a drop in the surplus from $236 billion in 2000 to $128 billion in 2001. The years after 2001 saw annual increases in spending, the deficit and consequently the debt.

These aforementioned factors also contributed to the increase in the deficit (as a result of defense spending) in the following two years reaching $413 billion in 2004. The war in Iraq and the surge in health care costs dramatically changed federal spending from 2000 to 2010. According to information picked up at the website of the Heritage Foundation, the total deficits from 2011 to 2020 will amount to 13.65 trillion.

Table 5.10 Deficits and Total Debt, 2000-2010 (in billions) (16)

	2,000	2,010	2,015	2020
Annual Deficit	2,025	1,789	+236	5,629
Annual Debt	2,164	3,720	-1,555	14,456

As you can see in Table 5.10, revenue has stayed about the same since 2000, although spending has more than doubled. This adds money to the total debt, which in turn means that we pay more in interest on the debt every year.

The Role of Interest Expenditures

Issues surrounding interest payments on the debt complicate matters, and for that reason we take a look at what has become a significant part of federal spending. After thirty years of annual budget deficits, the federal government recorded four consecutive years of surpluses from 1998-2001, something that hadn't happened since before the Great Depression. However, these surpluses did little to dent the massive federal debt from the previous forty years. In fact, the surpluses were less than the net interest payments on the debt. (17)

How does interest weigh upon the federal debt? Net interest on the public debt was approximately $186.9 billion in 2009, or 5% of total spending. In that same year, the government also accrued a non-cash interest expense of $192 billion for intergovernmental debt, primarily the Social Security Trust Fund, for a total interest expense of $381 billion. (18) Interest is added to the Social Security Trust Fund and therefore the national debt each year and will be paid to Social Security recipients in the future. However, since it is a non-cash expense it is excluded from the budget deficit calculation.

Who Owns Our Debt? Public debt owned by foreigners has increased to approximately 50% of the total or approximately $3.4 trillion. As a result, almost 50% of the interest payments are now leaving the country, which is different from past years when interest was paid to U.S. citizens holding the public debt. The effect of interest payments going overseas is that money is invested overseas, not here.

How do falling interest payments affect debt payments? Net interest costs paid on the public debt went down from $242 billion in 2008 to $189 billion in 2009 because of lower interest rates. If these interest rates go back up to typical historical levels then so too will the annual interest payments. (19)

As you can see in table 5.10, the first five years of this decade have seen an unprecedented rise in spending, the deficit and the debt. Also worrisome are the projected numbers and entitlements that are scheduled to take effect in the coming years. As you can see in the chart below, spending and debt are becoming massive.

What's up with deficit for 2015 being so much lower than 2010? Of particular note in the chart is the much lower projected deficit. Although that number is very high, ($751.9 billion) it is considerably lower than what was incurred in 2010. ($1.55 trillion) Whether or not those deficit numbers come down is of key importance to the solvency of our nation.

Table 5.11 Deficit and Debt Predictions, 2010-2015 (in billions) (20)

	Revenue	Spending	Deficit	Total Debt
2010	2,164	3,720	-1,555	14,456
2015	3,633	4,385	-759	19,863

What is a good response to the extreme debt and deficit? We should consider basing our tax and budget policy on principles as opposed to projections. Time and time again, administrations and Congress have based spending and tax cuts on optimistic projections of revenue. The projections are based on factors that are impossible to predict. What happens so often is that revenues are lower than predicted, although the money for spending has already been allocated. Obviously this needs to change, which is the reason for the "Avenues to Progress" section below.

What are some dangers of this kind of debt? One would be an economic downturn in which tax revenues went down, in which case we would have a very hard time paying the bills. A second would be if lender countries no longer agreed to lend us more money.

Securing and Maximizing Social Security

A large percentage of Americans are counting on Social Security as a part of their retirement, although there are issues with the functionality of the system, a few of which we look at here.

Why is it incredibly important that we look at our Social Security System now? This system has to work if we are going to prevent elderly poverty and preserve quality of life for Americans in their old age. The hard part is that we have to worry not just about "fixing" Social Security, but also maintaining the long-term solvency of our government.

How much of the budget is Social Security spending? In 2010 Social Security spending was 20% of the budget, or $678 billion, primarily funded through a dedicated payroll tax. However, that number is expected to rise due to the impending retirement of those born in the fifties and sixties.

Social Security spending is projected to rise from 4.8% of GDP in 2010 to 5.9% of GDP by 2030, where it will plateau. Payments will then exceed revenues and according to some, the trust funds will be exhausted by 2037, (21) although there are many, many different opinions on that.

What is the "payouts to revenue" and "workers to recipients ratio?" In 2010, the government paid out $686 billion with revenue of $807 billion, for a surplus of $121 billion. However, as the number of recipients grows in comparison to those paying in, the system becomes harder to maintain. As of 2010, 2.94 workers paid in per 1 benefits recipient. 156 million paid in, 53 million received benefits. However, the problem develops when the number of recipients begins to exceed the number of people paying in. (20)

What is the relationship between social security and health care costs? When health care costs rise, people on fixed incomes suffer. There are many opinions on how to "fix" Social Security, but controlling health care prices is one point we should be able to agree on. That's because those of us on fixed incomes simply can't handle sharp increases in monthly health care premiums. The chart below shows average 2010 payouts; try to imagine the effect that rising health care prices could have on this budget.

Table 5.12 Social Security 2010 Payout Statistics (21)

Average Annual Payout to Retired Couples (2010)	$22,704
Average monthly payment to a retired worker	$1,177

What would the precise effect of increased health care costs on retired couples be? As you can see above, the average annual payout to retired couples in 2010 was $22,704, so any increase in health care costs could be devastating.

How can the media help us to secure and maximize the system work? We need the media to take on the issue of securing Social Security through a series of op-eds., round tables and other tactics to engage the people. Hope for this came to me from the decision of one Northeastern professor and Fox 25 Boston to engage twenty-five journalism students in multi-media projects. If more universities follow the lead of Northeastern, then our media will experience a surge in its capacity to lead initiatives to protect Social Security.

Do any ideas in education relate to maximizing our revenues and with it Social Security? Yes, supporting vocational education. We need to rebuild our manufacturing base to rebuild the economy and protect revenues, but for that we need skilled workers, which is why we need more vocational education.

AVENUES TO PROGRESS

I hope that the tables, information and perspectives in this chapter have been interesting to you. However, what I'm really interested in is solutions ion how we can do better, how different entities can work together to promoting the policies that will lead to a healthy and sustainable future.

How do we build the tools for transparency? This book advocates the creation of a "Citizen's Book," a work that can allow Americans to better understand their government. However, there are excellent existing tools available, such as the *People's Guide to the Federal Budget*, put out by the National Priorities Project. The publications of the Mercatus Center at George Mason University also offer insight and feedback of the work of federal agencies; you can browse their online library.

What kind of analysis do we need on college campuses? As powerful as the greater tools of transparency may be, what we really need is analysis of spending and policies from both a fiscal and moral perspective. Chapter Eight focuses on the role college campuses can play in winning the Green Revolution, although of course federal spending is another area for college campuses to lead in. The website of the *Committee for a Responsible Federal Budget* has a deficit reduction planning tool for the classroom.

What is a good model for engagement by local media that could help in discussion of federal polices? In early 2015, a journalism class at Northeastern University partnered with Fox 25 to do a series of investigative journalism pieces on stories that affected people in Massachusetts. For those interested in reversing the downward spiral we seem to be in this country, this model is huge; if imitated it can provide the manpower and passion that is so desperately needed if we are to find solutions to our complicated challenges. At a time when local papers in Massachusetts are hopelessly understaffed, this model brings hope. (22)

What is an example of good budget analysis in the classroom? One December 5, 2013 article in Forbes told the story of a University of Georgia class studying the federal budget. Titled "Balancing the Federal Budget; So Easy a Class of College Students Can Do It," the article tells the story of fifteen weeks students spent looking at options for getting the budget under control.

What are some good PBS movies on the subject of federal spending? Watching every movie I could find on PBS about the American situation has paid dividends and taught me principles that are relevant to this chapter. Perhaps most helpful was the movie "740 Park", part of the "Why Poverty" series. That movie emphasized just how out of control lobbyists in Washington are, in practice stripping the American people of our future. The movie should be watched in the classroom, analyzed and reviewed by local papers, then discussed by town meetings. In short, dismantling the vice grip of lobbyists on our future will help return control of spending to the people, but for that we need to work together.

What is a model from the past that could work well now? Created from a grant by the Pew Charitable Trust, the group *Americans Discuss Social Security* is a group that "focuses on engaging American citizens in discussing the reformation of the United States Social Security System." What's exciting about that model is the deep, far reaching way in which the group engaged hundreds of thousands of Americans, including town meetings, which in my opinion is one of the strongest institutions we have for creating stability and change. We should bring back that model for discussion in our local papers.

. . .

Chapter Five Questions

1. What are the five principal areas of federal spending?

2. What is the difference between mandatory and discretionary spending?

3. What are the top mandatory spending categories?

4. Defense spending is very high; can you think of some peaceful activities our military might engage in?

5. What does the paragraph "principles versus projections" emphasize?

6. According to the author, what are two important aspects of making Social Security work?

7. How could the federal government better promote fiscal transparency?

8. What do you think of our existing transparency tools? How can we best engage the public?

9. How can we best integrate our colleges and universities into the debate?

10. Which of the "avenues to progress" did you like best?

6

Simplifying the Federal Tax System

"the flat tax would be so simple, you could fill it out on a post card...It would be honest. It would eliminate the principal source of political corruption in Washington — trading loopholes for campaign cash. It would be fair." (1)

-Steve Forbes

This chapter seeks to demonstrate why simplification of the federal tax code could do a great deal to improve the situation of many Americans. Being able to do our taxes quickly and easily is only one of the benefits. True simplification can make the workings of the government easier to understand, discourage tax evasion, make the work of tax accountants easier, allow IRS agents the time to focus on other problems, promote greater transparency and as a consequence assure that our tax dollars are spent wisely. So, the goal of this article is to expand upon the multiple ways we can become a healthier nation through slowly moving toward a one bracket, no exemption federal tax system.

The simplification of the federal tax system hasn't happened yet means that both taxpayers and IRS agents suffer. Taxpayers suffer from time and stress spent filing and IRS agents are bogged down by complicated tax codes. This is especially true since 2010. "During FY 2010, the IRS encountered many challenges, including a variety of tax provisions that were created, extended, or expanded. There were over 100 new provisions alone just from the American Recovery and Reinvestment Act and the Patient Protection and Affordable Care Act." (2) However, these latest complications are just the tip of the iceberg.

Is the stress of taxpayers and IRS agents not reason enough for simplification? I think it is. The amount of stress, time and money spent on federal tax returns could be more wisely spent responding to other pressing needs. This is not mentioning the pressures IRS agents can be put under, including forms of intimidation that are more possible in the age of the Internet. IRS agents need to be able to do their job without fear, anything else just isn't fair.

Chapter Six Concerns

A. GOVERNMENT IS EASIER TO UNDERSTAND.-K.I.S.S. so we all can discuss the matter and not be lead into the conversation by half-truths.

B. SIMPLICITY REDUCES TAX EVASION-Complication breeds dishonesty and confusion.

C. FLAT TAX IS BUSINESS FRIENDLY- Add man hours to making money and not on how to hide it.

D. WHERE IS THERE PROGRESS- Where and how is the conversation changing.

. . .

Government is Easier to Understand

A flat tax makes the workings of the government more understandable to the people. For many of us, the system is so complicated that when politicians debate tax policy it's hard to tell who's right. For example, recently I saw politicians on TV debating the effects of a tax cut. Both sides made claims that I found out to be half-truths; contrary to first year economics. The first politician claimed that 60% of the tax cuts would benefit the top 5%. What's so deceptive about that? The top 5% contributes almost 60% of federal tax revenue (see chart below), so cutting taxes the same percentage across the board would mean that the upper 5% would receive 60% of the benefits. (3) The other politician claimed the government would get all tax cut money back in revenues, as the economy would be stimulated by investments caused by cuts.

What is a better way to talk about tax policy? We need new authors, journalists and college classrooms to analyze and write about tax issues. They are the only trump card to restricting discussion of tax policy to the political sphere. As Einstein said; "those who are concerned with the triumph of justice and reason need to be keenly aware how little influence these bear in the political sphere." This is why we need analysis outside the political sphere.

Table 6.1 Who Pays Taxes? (4)

Percentiles Ranked by Income	Income Thresholds on Percentiles	Percentage of Federal Personal Income Tax Paid
Top 1%	$343,927	36.73
Top 5%	$154,643	58.66
Top 10%	$112, 124	70.47
Top 25%	$66,193	87.30
Top 50%	$32,396	97.75

Source: IRS

What is a statement regarding who pays taxes, this chart and fairness that I feel should be integrated into the conversation? Much of discussion of tax policy devolves to how the system benefits the super rich and is inherently unfair. Whether or not that is true, *what is true* in my experience is that not enough Americans of modest means get to experience the natural wonders of America. The wealthy have country clubs and the cash to fly to and access to national parks, but we need to make it easier for everyone to.

How can the super rich help in the creation of a green infrastructure that everyone can enjoy? There is a national park that some are working to create and protect the natural wonders of Maine (5) (and with it New England), not to mention five other national parks that could be created nationwide. (6) I do believe that the more fortunate owe it to everyone to help make this happen.

What might be a good, transparent system of taxation that is fair to everyone? If we all paid a 25% federal income tax; any increase or lowering of taxes would be *easy for everyone to understand.* We would be able to more easily discuss tax rates without the confusion that currently plagues such conversations now. I believe that this ease of discussion would lead to more transparent, understandable government.

Simplicity Reduces Tax Evasion

Tax evasion would be far more difficult if the system was simpler. With a one bracket no exemptions structure, the IRS *would have the time* to make sure that everyone was paying what is due. Why do we have to make things so hard and complicated? It was once said that "income taxes make more liars of out of men than golf," although I believe that a one bracket, flat income tax could go a long way to make tax time easier, not mention stop the trend of making criminals out of otherwise honest Americans.

Flat Tax is Business Friendly

In a March 2009 article in *The Libertarian*, Richard Epstein argues; "In the private sector, a flat tax reduces the distortions that otherwise arise when two individuals receive different after-tax returns on their labor or investment. The flat tax also eliminates private incentives to concoct wasteful schemes to shift their income onto the ledger of their poorer relatives." (7) In other words, simplicity of tax codes is good for honest family relations.

What are attitudes toward the flat tax outside the U.S.? Outside United States there has been a flat tax revolution. "On January 1, 2001, Russia joined the Baltic states with a rate of only 13% (the country's corporate tax is still very high). Because of President Vladimir Putin's act, "tax reform jump started Russia's economy and tax revenue skyrocketed, doubling within three years." (8) In the case of Russia, perhaps the fact that *everyone had to pay* that rate put pressure on the wealthy that had long been avoiding paying.

Business Advantages of a Flat Tax

The first advantage to business is that simpler filings naturally are easier for businesses to do. The second advantage is that distortions and schemes are harder to pull off, simply because of the simple nature of the filings. Third, the transparency that results from the simplicity of the system means that dishonest businesses are less likely to maintain a competitive advantage over honest ones because of tax fraud games and deceit. That alone is reason to change. Finally, the simplicity of the income or corporate tax rate can be something that all businesses have in common. In my opinion this is one way to bind business owners together. Perhaps that can help them accept a bit more of a "common fate" and bring them closer to the sort of collectivist problem-solving approach that is needed at both the business and government levels.

Steve Forbes and the Flat Tax

A number of years ago Steve Forbes ran for president on the platform of simplifying the tax system and reducing the percentage to 17%. It would be a great thing to establish the one bracket system, but perhaps the fact that his plan included significantly reduced revenues made the concept more than the government could handle. This is especially true given our large federal debt. However, the efforts of Steve Forbes to simplify the tax system have provided us with some research and writings on this subject, efforts that just may pay dividends down the line.

Where is There Progress

Although the overall advantage of federal tax simplification is huge, educating the public about the advantages of this is a lot of work. In my experience there are two main myths to be confronted. The first myth is that a flat tax is not friendly to families or business, and the second is that this will keep the wealthy from paying.

Is a flat tax good for working families? I'm inclined to believe that few things would be better for working families than a one bracket, no exceptions federal income tax. First of all, simplification would be a big step toward greater understanding of our federal government, something we all need. Second, a one bracket system could more easily be adapted to lessen the burden of working families by raising the threshold at which we can begin to pay. As the table "Who Pays Taxes" demonstrates, only 4.4% of federal income tax revenue comes from the lower half of earners, so lifting some of the burden from that group would not significantly decrease revenue.

What does Steve Forbes have to say? As Steve Forbes once said; "Since 1970 — in just 25 years — Washington spending has increased more than seven fold. During those same years, family income in America has declined. But the politicians say "we" can't afford a tax cut." (9) Who knows, maybe with some tax simplification and subsequent spending cuts we will be able to cut our tax rates, but I wouldn't bank on it.

Do the rich pay taxes? One of the misconceptions that a lot of people have is that members of the highest income bracket don't pay any taxes, when in fact the top five percent of earners contribute more than 70% of federal tax revenues. As one expert said: "In 2006, the top quintile of households earned 55.7 percent of pretax income and paid 69.3 percent of federal taxes, while the top 1 percent of households earned 18.8 percent of income and paid 28.3 percent of taxes." (9) What that means is that you could argue that as a whole, America's top 1% is paying their share. That said, there are other areas of inequality to focus on, such as injustices created by the system of lobbyists, explained in the next question.

What might be a better area of fairness to focus on than rich people paying more taxes? Reducing the influence of lobbyists in favor of the people Washington is a necessary step forward, the importance of which was made clear in the PBS "Why Poverty" series. (10) I had often heard about how lobbyists in Washington have too much power, but I hadn't realized just how true this was until I saw the movie "740 Park" on *PBS* (available on their online movies). One of the movies in the "Why Poverty" series, "740 Park" portrays the grim reality of how the political system does not favor the common man. In short, worrying about how much the top 1% pay is a good area to look at, but even better would be to look at how to return control of Washington away from the lobbyists and back into the control of the voters.

How should we go about creating the most fair tax system possible? We want to engage as many people as possible in the debate, including new authors, journalists and college classrooms. That is, new authors need to write books about new aspects of tax policy and college classrooms need to be reading and debating that policy.

What's an outside the box idea for starting off discussion of positive tax policy on college campuses? Before college classrooms talk about the ways to improve tax policy, they need to commit to having the discussion in a different way. One way could be to sing "This is Your Land" by Woody Guthrie as a class. What song can better evoke the best spirit of America? What is a better way to bring out the best in people, singing in harmony together? Myself, although I love the Woody Guthrie version of the song, my favorite is that sung by the Solidarity Project in Wisconsin; they bring out the spirit of the song and have a great time doing it.

What's another way to engage college students and other members of the younger generation in the debate on tax policy? Maybe IRS agents could go to classrooms, talk about changes in tax law from their perspective and talk about what could or couldn't be done better. Maybe they could talk about more serious concerns they have, such as the dangers of a complex tax system creating an environment in which intimidation could thrive. Some might shy away from the idea of college students discussing such a subject, but I think the young people have a right to the truth; only then do they have a chance to make things better for themselves.

One thing I've found researching this book is that most of our problems are not that complex. We just need to communicate, work together and progress. As the sign in the locker room of the 1993 Boston College Football team locker room said; "Lead, Follow or Get Out of the Way."

What is a bright ray of hope for greater contributions by the media to figuring out solutions to fairness and equality on then subject of tax policy and everything else? The brightest ray of hope I've learned about with regard to the quality of analysis of public policy is the decision of Fox 25 Boston to employ twenty-five Northeastern students to do investigative journalism pieces. With that move, the number of qualified investigative journalists in Massachusetts just went up exponentially. I'm particularly sensitive to this fact, in part from running for office on a platform (including tax simplification concepts) that the media was either unwilling or unable to address. However, with the rank of journalists continuing to grow, future candidates for office (but not me) may find the journalistic manpower they need to push productive discussions of tax policy into the fore, which, if people attention, has the power to positively impact quality of life for all Americans.

. . .

Chapter Six Questions

1. What are five positive effects of simplifying the federal tax system?
2. Which is the best argument for a simplified tax system?
3. Do think tax simplification would result in less fraud?
4. How much time did you spend doing your income tax return last year?
5. Could federal tax simplification make the job of tax accountants easier?
6. Were you surprised by anything you saw in Table 6.1; "Who Pays Taxes?"
7. Do you think a simplified tax system could result in less intimidation of IRS agents?
8. What do you think of connecting the responsibilities of the 1% to an expansion of the national park system?
9. What role do you think investigative journalism students like those at Northeastern University can play in the future of tax simplification?
10. Do you see a link between tax simplification and greater transparency and responsibility on the part of our federal government?

7

Building Health and Well-being

"If health fails, teaching, knowledge, life itself, all comes to naught. So have nothing to do with alcohol and avoid all things against which the conscience speaks."

-Ras Tafari

100 Days of Progress

This chapter exists because I believe many Americans can enjoy life more through systematically building their well-being. In my language teaching I always emphasize two steps; 1) Define your goals and the elements of making progress that go into reaching them. And, 2) Figure out a program that will allow you to make progress every day. Then, carry out this program for 100 days. When you make progress *every day*, there is no pressure to rush.

Chapter Seven Concerns

A. CORE PRINCIPALS- Three important factors for good health.

B. GRIM STATISTICS ON PHYSICAL AND MENTAL HEALTH-A check up on the American people.

C. QUESTIONS FOR NEW AUTHORS, JOURNALISTS, COLLEGE CLASSROOMS AND YOU TO ANALYZE AND EXPAND UPON- 26 questions about our health and our communities health.

...

Core Principals

In order for more people to systematically build their health, we need to look at three core principles that support the process of us feeling our best; 1) the right mind set, 2) the role of necessary supports and 3) the importance of friends and community. Part of the role of this chapter is to recognize each of these three elements and how we can help insure that they are working for people.

The First Core Principle

Grasping the three core principles, mind set and having someone to share and reach health goals with, are what will enable the application of the ideas and information. The first core belief was the importance of mind set; that is, that we need the right mind set before effectively applying the ideas. This is a fact that I learned from studying jui-jitsu, a Japanese grappling art. I realized that success in the art was not about any specific techniques. Rather, it was about committing to the right mind set, after which the techniques would come naturally. By the same token, there are tons of ideas and tactics for building health, but I believe that people will only utilize them when they are ready, when they have the right mind set.

The Second Core Principle

The second core principle was the realization of the crucial role that new authors, college campuses that engage in problem-solving and healthy local newspapers need to play to create our better health. We need all of them to succeed in building a better world. The good news is that these three entities seem to be evolving and filling our need for good information. The most recent example of this I'm aware of was the decision of Fox25 to employ twenty-five Northeastern students in doing investigative journalism.

The Third Core Principle

The third surprise was the most important principle I found; the fact that having someone to share and reach health goals with is one of the most powerful tools of all. This is a fact I learned from the *Rushey Green Time Bank* in England, a 55+ time bank in England. As the case study of this time bank tells us, one doctor decided to use the time bank system to help his patients support each other in their quest for better health. They found that these relationships had a huge positive impact on the physical and mental health of time bank members. (1) Not everyone wants to join a time bank, but it's good to remember the principle of the value of friends and community in building health.

Grim Statistics on Physical and Mental Health

Before going into some of the specific ideas on building health, it's important to too many Americans are in a daily battle for their health and are being robbed of opportunities to enjoy life to the fullest. The statistics below represent a few of the grim indicators.

- 65% of Americans take prescription medications daily, 43% are mood altering. (2)
- "Forty million Americans in the U. S. will experience an impairment because of an anxiety condition this year. Only four million of those diagnosed with a stress or anxiety condition will receive treatment. Of those, only 400,000 will receive proper treatment." (3)
- According to a 2009 report, "Chronic Pain affects an estimated 70 million Americans....ongoing pain can also undermine overall physical, psychological and social well-being, and is a major cause of disability and costly health care utilization." (4)
- An estimated 26.2 percent of Americans ages 18 and older — about one in four adults — suffer from a diagnosable mental disorder in a given year. Some might argue that diagnosing mental health is a subjective science, but the fact is that their quality of life is being disrupted. (5)
- The number of Americans reporting extreme stress continues to be high; 20 percent said their stress in an 8, 9 or 10 on a 10-point scale. (6)
- From 1999 to 2010, the suicide rate among Americans ages 35 to 64 rose by nearly 30 percent, to 17.6 deaths per 100,000 people, up from 13.7. (7)

Table 7.1: The Multiple Entities in 100 Days of Progress Building Health

New Authors,Universities & Local Papers	We need new authors to explore the health themes of this chapter in greater depth, local papers that look at how readers might benefit and colleges that engage in analysis and problem-solving
Share & Reach Goals With Friends	As I learned from the Rushey Green Time Bank, having someone to share and reach goals with is very important. Together people can build the right mind set, after which exploration of the health themes happens naturally.

Questions for New Authors, Journalists, College Classrooms and You to Analyze and Expand Upon

The following questions and answers are largely a collection of expert opinions; I have gleaned the most important points but I encourage readers to go to the original articles, which can be found in the End Notes.

1. How have I applied the principle of having friends to share and reach health goals with? Having a friend to share and reach health goals with. I learned this from reading about the success stories of *Rushey Green Time Bank*, in which physician created a group that facilitated these sorts of partnerships. (8) Imagine the difference between an older person trying to figure out how to build their health alone with two people that share and reach their goals together. Big difference!

Within the Rushey Green Time Bank (for people 55+) in England, members encouraged each other to reach their health goals through sharing information with each other about doctors, medications, personal trainers, workouts or anything else.

2. How have I applied the principle of making a little progress every day? Make just a little bit of progress every day for one hundred days. I'm a language teacher and always tell my students to do exactly that; figure out a daily study routine that will make you better and then do it for one hundred days. The same system can be used for building health; find five or six aspects of health and then work at those aspects every day. This is effective because it takes the pressure off; daily progress means you can slow down, have fun and do things the right way.

3. What are some specific benefits of strength training? According to Even minimal training can improve skin healing, prevent the need for estrogen therapy in women, help memory and teeth, and prevent Alzheimer's and dementia, among many other benefits. (9) The trick is to do this safely and effectively; for which we are going to need more people with the training and certification to teach people how to work out. This is especially true with older people; because there is a real lack of trainers with the qualifications, training and certifications to work with older people. It seems to me that this is something our colleges and universities need to address by responding with the appropriate coursework. (10) Another response is for more personal trainers to get training and certification to work with older people, which can happen through individual gyms insisting on having one trainer with elderly certification.

4. Why do some insist that older people need to focus on "correcting deficits" before dealing with wider health issues? According to one "Senior Sister," a large number of older people living in nursing homes are dehydrated or suffer from malnutrition. According to the same source, the problem is that the symptoms of malnutrition or dehydration can often be mistaken for psychosis or other problems. As one "Senior Sister" said; "if your relative suddenly starts to hear voices, noises and develop delusional thinking, investigations need to be made before any psychiatric label is given." (11)

When reading about this, my first thought is to apply the same principle from the work of Rushey Green Time Bank of having a friend to share and reach health goals with. Family and friends also need to be aware of this phenomenon to help assure that nursing home residents are eating and drinking enough. (12) However, mentioning that here really isn't good enough; this is something that needs to be addressed by authors in books and in turn read and analyzed by college classrooms.

A casual search on Google reveals that Western Carolina is one such college that offers coursework by and "in collaboration with the World Health Organization." (13)

5. Why is the role of healthy, locally grown food to health? What can we do as individuals and as a society to promote this? Everyone needs access to healthy food to feel their best, preserve and even build their health. Simply put, you have to give your body the nutrients it needs. There are four main approaches to giving people that access.

First, farmer's markets gets healthy produce to customers while being a good place for farmers and consumers to connect.

Second, buying shares in Community Supported Agriculture provides customers with a weekly supply of produce while reducing risk for the farmer, because he gets paid early in the season. (14)

Third, serving healthy, locally grown food in the schools can indirectly help seniors, because it supports the farms and can lead the way to doing the same in the senior living centers.

Fourth, we should be able to buy fresh food and vegetables at stores near us, as opposed to being forced to get in the car. This is especially true for seniors. We should work toward having convenience stores that stock fresh produce, ideally within walking distance.

6. How do we improve the "green infrastructure" for us to live healthier? We need to continue to improve and expand our walking and bike paths through the application of three successful models; rail trails, the *Safe Routes* walk-to-school programs and models for improving community green infrastructure profiled on the website pedbikeinfo.org. Individually, each of three approaches to building green infrastructure are powerful; Another aspect of improving green infrastructure is an expansion of the national parks system. In my view, the national parks are too few. Mostly concentrated in the West, there have been few additions to the park system in recent years.

However, one wonderful project that we need to make a priority is the Maine Woods project, one that will set aside 3.4 million acres of wilds in Northern Maine. For New Englanders, this could be the capstone that to all other conservation efforts, because we can know it's part of a larger plan to preserve our wild places and healthy lifestyle.

For me, learning about the Maine North Woods project was exciting, because it can streamline well with the world peace goals of this book. How? Through utilizing the Veterans Conservation Corp. for maintenance and upkeep of parks. I had long advocated the idea of converting defense spending into spending on building our green infrastructure, but didn't know how that would work. The Veterans Conservation Corp. employs returning veterans in conservation projects, but it seems that their funding is limited; but what a perfect place to move defense spending to! After all, it would be a win/win; veterans could have employment to allow them to readjust to civilian life and we could watch our national parks grow and flourish. I for one hole onto the dream of seeing that happen.

7. What is an outside the box example of expression for families and communities to connect? My favorite is the "seven generations" tradition of the Alabama-Coushatta, a Texas Native American tribe. In their society, every important question at hand is discussed in terms of how it impacts the dreams of the previous seven generations and coming seven generations. (15) This practice can take discussions to a whole new level of emotional range and scope, which can be especially important for people to break out of frustrating, limited discussions.

8. What is the relationship between exercise and aging? What college offers curriculum to help with this? According to a 1998 *New York Times* article, several studies indicate that getting aerobic exercise and maintaining proper nutrition, while important, are not sufficient to protect people's aging bodies. "The research has made clear," says the article, "that working to restore muscle strength and bone density is crucial in realizing the potential for a healthy old age." (16) So, big deal, but what can we do with this information? Ideally, we can engage our colleges and universities in educating people to work out the right way; to maximize life as we get older. To repeat the theme in question seven, curriculum similar to that offered by Western Carolina is a step in the right direction.

'Until the age of thirty, the bones of both males and females grow and become thicker. After that they very gradually become thinner and weaker. The degree of this thinning varies greatly, but everyone experiences it to some degree. The condition known as osteoporosis occurs when bones become too thin and prone to breaking easily. This is especially common among older women, for whom injuries from osteoporosis are a major cause of disability.' (17)

9. How do I offset the thinning of bones? According to information on *The Walking Site*, the only way to offset this gradual thinning is by placing consistent resistance on the muscles, tendons and bones. Although walking has many positive health benefits, walking alone isn't enough to make up for the effects of osteoporosis. The only way to offset the thinning is through strength training, combined with a good diet that includes plenty of vitamin D and calcium. (18) *The New York Times* provides timely and detailed information;

"Strength training helps strengthen muscles and bones in your arms and upper spine, and weight-bearing exercises—such as walking, jogging, running, stair climbing, skipping rope, skin and impact-producing sports—mainly affect the bones in your legs, hips and lower spine." (19)

So, we know that strength training can be good for people, but what remains in my mind are so many questions; what books have been written on this subject? Are there any college classrooms studying how older people in their community can benefit from strength training? What work is being done to assure that more personal trainers are receiving the proper training and certification to effectively help older people?

10. What is the role of tendons and can I strengthen them? In the words of "Tendons are connective tissues that help attach muscles to bones, and are an essential part of our musculoskeletal structure that requires correct use and maintenance. According to the *New York Times* "it is imperative for people to systematically and proactively build their health through the best possible food and exercise," including exercise and strengthening of the tendons." (20) The problem is most people don't think to work out the tendons, which is yet another reason for more education on resistance training like the coursework offered at Western Carolina, mentioned on

11. What can I do to promote heart health for young and old? According to an article in , "So many things we do to help our heart, like quitting smoking, eating more fiber, and moving more, also help other parts of our body, including our bones, colon, lungs, and skin," (21) According to WebMD, regular exercise "can strengthen your heart and cardiovascular system, improve circulation and help your body use oxygen better, lower blood pressure, increase energy, reduce stress, tension, anxiety and depression and make you feel more relaxed and rested." (22)

12. What is the relationship of stretching and coordination to balance? When I was twelve years old, I watched my eighty-five year old grandfather fall onto the pavement in front of *Old South Church* in Boston and break his hip. It was a devastating injury from which he never really recovered. Nor is he alone; every year many Americans take falls that will change their lives for their worse. This is one reason why it is crucial to have core information on ways that older people can maintain flexibility and coordination. Many understand how coordination can help to lessen the chance of falling, but it seems that fewer understand just how correlated coordination is with flexibility. According to Home Fitness Essentials, "There is some evidence that stretching can prevent injuries, at least if done properly. Maintaining some degree of flexibility can also help with keeping your posture healthy, reducing back pain, and balance." (24) What this tells me is simple; as in so many other cases we need authors, journalists, college classrooms and local papers exploring this idea in depth.

13. Can Tai Chi help with coordination? A study by the *National Institute of Aging* looked at the effects of Tai Chi on older adults, and found that "consistent Tai Chi practice significantly reduces fear of falling among older adults." While it might sound odd at first to talk about the benefits of reducing fear instead of reducing the rate of falling itself, in fact the fear of falling has been positively linked to increased numbers of actual falls, because fear "leads to gait alteration, deconditioning, less participation in activities and social interaction, and a worse self-perception of health." (25)

The effect of Tai Chi on older people is of personal interest to me because my father has issues with his balance. When he was younger he used to stumble occasionally, but it wasn't a serious problem, because he never hurt himself. Now that he's older, I worry more and even suggested that he look into practicing Tai Chi. His doctor suggested the same thing, although at first even the beginning Tai Chi moves were hard for him. However, he is working diligently through a program at the Tufts Medical School to improve his balance to the point where he can eventually participate in the Tai Chi classes.

14. Can strength building reduce injury? According to WebMd. , a good layer of muscle all over the body can help to minimize the debilitating impact of falls, hard work, or any other stress. (26) This is fairly common knowledge, but fewer people realize that building muscle can help with flexibility. According to preliminary research posted on WebMD, "Our results suggest that full-range resistance training regimens can improve flexibility as well as, or perhaps better than, typical static stretching regimens." (27)

15. Why do older people need professionals with special training and certification? I know that I would love to see a few older people close to me systematically build up the strength and flexibility in every part of their body, but the trick is find the professionals with the training and experience to do it. This is where the need for more special certification for those working older people comes in, as outlined in question eight. (28)

One recent study found that "deep-breathing relaxation techniques can help patients cope with pain and anxiety during a medical procedure following coronary bypass surgery." (29) The question is; how many people have had training in this? No one that I know; maybe if this sort of practical information was taught more at the university level, more would have yet one more tool in their toolbox to improve their well-being.

16. How do we increase the opportunities for and benefits of walking? According to *The Walking Site*, "for cardio benefits the key is walking fast enough to get your heart rate up." (30) However, also according to the Walking Site, 'as healthy as walking is, on its own it doesn't provide some of the benefits that strength training and intense aerobic training do.' "You can improve your appearance, strength, muscle to fat ratio, and even your walking performance by adding strength training to your walking routine." (31)

For older people to have opportunities to walk, Chapters Three and Nine offer approaches to systematically to build our network of walking and biking options. The growth of rail trails, Safe Routes models and goals of groups like Pedbike Info (pedbikeinfo.org) can help both younger and older Americans with environments to enjoy, connect and build their health.

17. How can time banks help older, isolated and poor people achieve better health? First, time exchanges can provide people with essential services. Second, receiving some services without paying can and free up capital for other investments in health, such as buying better food or making more visits to a trusted doctor. Some health clinics even accept time dollars as payment, such as *The True North Health Clinic* in Portland, Maine. Members can also use time dollars for services that are just not part of the traditional economy, such as one member sharing their experiences and knowledge of a medication of health care plan with another member. (32)

A doctor of the Rushey Green Time Bank in England also said;

'Time banking can help people become healthy by giving them shared goals, such as becoming active in their communities, taking exercise classes, participating in health promotion activities (e.g., healthy eating courses, and accessing support to meet personal goals.') (33)

If the sorts of benefits that time banks can bring sound interesting to you, then have a look at the websites of the time bank umbrella organization Hour World. Their interactive map can tell you what time banks are near you.

18. Can we utilize historical perspective in our health crisis? The discussions on health in Washington and in our media are too political and lack almost completely in spirituality. This is nothing new. Perhaps this sort of "everything but what's actually helpful approach" inspired the 1840's American Transcendentalist protests of the "arrogant intellectualism" at Harvard University and the corrupting influence of political parties. (34) In short, the people need to regain control of their health through lifestyle, healthy community and symbiotic relationships. Especially powerful would be if college classrooms across the country studied and debated this building from an economic and philosophical perspective. This is one of the themes of Chapter Eight; how colleges can contribute to a healthier, sustainable lifestyle.

19. Questions 11-20 contain so much material; how do we integrate all of this information? As is emphasized throughout the book, we need new authors, local newspapers and college classrooms to participate in the process of digesting this information. Still, there are many logistical questions as to how this is done; however, one answer comes to us from the *Northeastern School of Journalism*, where twenty-five writers will write articles and multimedia reports for Fox25 Boston. This is a gamechanger; with the added support of students in covering our complicated, ever changing world, community papers can focus on how their papers integrate timely health information, such as that in the previous ten questions, into their community.

20. What documentaries on food and well-being do you like? One of the new assets for people and the planet we live on are the wide range of high quality videos on food, health the environment and local economies. Signing up for Netflix and gaining access to these documentaries was one of the best things I ever did. The movies *Food Matters* (35) or *Forks Over Knives* (36) were a really good start and helped educate me to look in the right places to find solutions. Without the understanding that many of our problems are systemic, the grim health statistics would have been only a source of confusion, not enlightenment.

21. What is an example of an imbalance in our culture that may lead to poor health? Our total lack of respect for those animals qualified as "food animals." I believe that we suffer from high levels of stress, depression and disease in part because of the terrible suffering that "food animals" endure.

22. How are low testosterone levels a canary in the coal mine? Many males in America now suffer from low testosterone levels, the symptoms of which are irritability, a decrease in muscle mass and bone density (which can lead to osteoporosis) lower sex drive, and difficulty concentrating. (37) The problem is that there seems to be little public awareness of this, which may be why we hear little talk of solutions, apart from "testosterone therapy," or drug use to bring up low levels.

Low estrogen levels among women are also a problem, with similar symptoms; irritability, mood swings and panic attacks. (38) What should be abundantly clear is the need for us to ask all the hard questions as to what chemicals in our environment might be responsible for these problems. Again, this is where we need the trifecta of new authors, journalists and college classrooms engaged in problem-solving to deal with this issue.

23. Have we made any progress in how we address our environmental problems? I don't think so. In the 1950's Rachel Carson was attacked relentlessly for her book Silent Spring, which warned of the dangers of DDT (an anti-pest chemical in extensive use) on the environment. By the same token, political candidates that talk about these issues are likely ignored by the mainstream media. However, the seriousness of our environmental problems requires a look at what's going on in our farms, cities and wild places. One place to start could be to look at issues surrounding the declining bee population.

24. How can jui-jitsu help people build their health? Now I base my workouts on time, not repetitions. I use a timer to four minute "rounds" with a thirty second break in between. During those four minutes rounds I do a variety of exercises, including push-ups, crunches, squats, kettle bell swings, medicine ball tosses, shadow boxing, crawls, pull ups or just stretching. With a timer, the minutes can be broken in thirty or sixty second segments, either for variety or rest. I believe this time-based approach can help a lot of people feel better.

The ability of the body and mind to heal itself is remarkable, something that the "gentle art" has facilitated in me. What's remarkable is that I as a white belt have only scratched the surface of the well-being that the art brings.

25. Why is it important to eat more fruits and vegetables? What can communities do to help residents do this? According to Albert Einstein, "Nothing will increase human health and increase chances of survival on earth as much as the evolution to a vegetarian diet."(40) And, considering how many of our health problems are food related, we need to buy more vegetables at the market, shopping at farmer's markets or even buying a share in Community Supported Agriculture. One way to find fresh food near you is to check out the interactive map on the site of Local Harvest.

26. What role can a local economy play in health and wellness? A good network of walking and bike paths give us more options for healthy lifestyle choices. When children walk to school they can often focus better in their learning environment. Simply put, giving people the option to walk or bike instead of drive is one of the best things we can do for our individual and communal health. However, to implement the Pedestrian, Bike and Information Center Model, (41) we need to create the local experts that can aid in building the bike and walking friendly infrastructure. See Chapter Four for more on more on how to build healthy local economies.

. . .

Chapter Seven Questions

1. Were you surprised by any of the statistics on stress and depression?

2. Do you agree with the "possible causes" of stress, depression, and obesity put forward by this chapter?

3. What is the role of exercise for you?

4. Have you ever had any problems with stress or depression?

5. What did you think about table 8.1?

6. What is your take on the summer facilities model?

7. Before reading this article, what did you know about declining testosterone levels? What information was new?

8. Which of the ideas on "building community" can best fight stress and depression?

9. Do you think a time bank could help you in your life?

10. How large of an impact do you think time banks can have on the stress and depression of elderly, isolated people?

8

Building Peace and Progress on College Campuses

"Throughout modern history, students have been the engine that powers the most transformation of movements. From civil rights to women's rights, students acted as catalysts for earth shifting change."

- *Guide to Transforming your Campus, Community and Career, U.S. Green Building Council*

This chapter is founded on the premise that American colleges and universities are perfectly positioned to lead the Green Revolution and build a peaceful future for everyone. By "Green Revolution" I mean supporting local farms, building our network of walking and bike paths and developing safe, renewable sources of energy. I believe it will be young hearts that will lead this struggle.

In this chapter twenty-eight questions that colleges can ask and answer for themselves are proposed. We start by looking at some of the questions already being asked and answered in the name of "going green," then move to more "advanced" questions. When magazines or websites judge how "green" a college is, the criteria may include the number of solar panels, how well they recycle or if they are "carbon neutral." It is valuable to recognize these good things; other schools can learn from and perhaps even imitate the model. See Table 8.1. Other questions in the chapter focus on the classroom and field work questions that ambitious colleges can ask and answer.

Chapter Eight Concerns

A. ECONOMIC ADVANTAGES OF A BETTER ENERGY POLICY-What are the advantages?

B. QUESTIONS FOR A GREEN COLLEGE- 30 Questions to ponder.

. . .

Economic Advantages of a Better Energy Policy

Before looking at the great things our colleges can do, let's look at four general advantages of increasing our renewable energy use. First, we can invest some of the $300 billion we send overseas every year for oil here in green infrastructure. (1) Second, homes and businesses that produce at least some of their own power can save money and achieve a measure of self-reliance. Third, our air and environment will become cleaner, which can have a positive impact on our health and that of our wildlife, green spaces and farms. Fourth, we can be agents of peace in the world, because we won't have to worry so much about offending oil producing countries.

Table 8.1 Existing Measures of "Green" Colleges

Princeton Review of Green Colleges	Perhaps responding to the fact that 62% of students express interest in attending "green" colleges, the Princeton Review put out a manual ranking colleges' "greenness" on six criteria. A good place to start.
Campus Sustainability Best Practices Manual	Put out by the Massachusetts government, the CS Best Practices Manual is an easy-to-use guide for student bodies and colleges administrations to recognize and capitalize on green energy opportunities on campus.
AASHE	The American Association of Sustainability in Higher Education is arguably the leader in the nuts and bolts of building green campuses. Their website aashe.org and organizations provides leadership on 326 campuses.

Questions for a Green College

1. **How much food does the college buy from local producers?** Buying food from local farms is not only supporting the local economy, it also means more green space and a greater ability to have a personal relationship with the farm where the food comes

from. A relationship with local farmers means the university can better meet the health needs of students. Universities may also exercise ethical standards, such as insisting on the humane treatment of animals or not using pesticides.

The second reason for colleges and universities to buy food from local farmers is to stimulate the local economy. Along with supporting farmer's markets, buying shares of community supported agriculture and getting more local produce in the stores, schools and colleges buying their produce locally can help juice up local economies and give students the food they need to feel their best and prevent disease. Done right, there should be no shortage of summer student employment.

2. **Do students and faculty participate in crop mobs?** "Crop mobbing" is a good way for students to connect with local farms in a fun way. It's when groups of people go and help out farmers with their crops in return for a tour and maybe a good lunch after a morning's work. Mob jobs can include weeding, harvesting or any other job that can be done well by many hands.

   In Vermont, the Green Mountain Crop Mob is now linked with the University of Vermont Center for Sustainable Agriculture. Farmers can request to be put on the list through the UVM website, and students can sign up to be contacted about joining one of the mobs. It's a win-win situation for everyone.

3. **Is the food served at the college organic *and* humane?** By serving organic food on campus, community members are getting more nutrients and eating foods with fewer or no hormonal additives. Also, they are promoting more environmentally friendly farming methods and better treatment of livestock. Buying certified animal friendly, organic products means that it is *more likely* that the animals they came from were raised humanely and not fed drugs or hormones.

   The above opinion is a direct product of the movie *No Impact Man*, in which the main character takes the train to upstate New York to see a farm and understand how the food is grown. In the documentary, the farmer emphasized that you have to come see the animals for yourself to see how they're being treated. The only example of a class going to see how the animals are treated is a "Capstone class" at Boston Latin, (which I attended) who visited two slaughterhouses in Bridgewater and Dartmouth Ma.. (2) Although many might say that young people shouldn't be exposed to such things, I for one don't believe in sheltering people from the truth. Plus, since I went to Boston Latin back in the 1980's, I have noticed an increasingly disturbing trend in the American culture to cover up and gloss over the truth. This of course only leads to more suffering trapped under the lies and avoidance of reality. For this reason, kudos to the courageous participants in this field trip.

4. **Do campus members understand what "organic" means?** Organic farming is a return to farming that took place before the 19th and 20th century, a production method that better sustains the health of soils, ecosystems and people. Whereas modern agriculture would utilize artificial fertilizer, organic farms utilize crop rotation and "cover crops," planted to help to assure soil fertility and sustainability. Organic farmers emphasize weed suppression rather than weed killing pesticides, and avoid chemicals to combat pests. (3)

   Understanding organic labels is a good start, but to effectively support the healthiest approaches to farming, there also needs to be a real relationship between farmers and consumers. Learning about the organic label is a start, but an Environmental Studies class might also look at whether students have the option to eat organically grown foods at the school cafeteria.

5. **What percentage of energy used on campus in produced by the college?** A growing number of colleges produce some of their own power from solar panels, solar water heaters, wind turbines and other mechanisms. Colleges that produce at least some of their own energy are more self-reliant and take pressure off of the grid. Additionally, these campus energy mechanisms can serve as learning tools to understand energy.

   A good example of this kind of reliance is Butte College in Northern California, which in 2011 became the first American college to be "grid positive;" producing more electricity than it consumes. The 25,000 solar panels produce a surplus that can power hundreds of homes as well. Even better, the college is on track to save millions in energy costs down the road. (4) Of course not every college has the access to solar radiance that they have in Northern California, but every school can work toward the goal while including community members in the learning process.

6. **How is the recycling program?** Most campuses have recycling programs, but some incorporate elements that other campuses do not, such as recycling steel. One way to measure how well schools are doing is to participate in the annual RecycleMania competition. Success is measured in part by "recyclable pounds per person," with each college getting a rating. The feedback from this friendly competition can help lead to idea sharing and advancements in recycling. (5)

   So, having a recycling competition is a good start, but just as this chapter is about expanding the ways to judge how "green" a campus is, so too can greater analysis of the effectiveness of the recycling program; new analyses can include looking at how leaves and other yard waste is recycled on campus grounds. To be truly progressive, one might look at all three words involved in increasing utilization of resources; reduce, reuse, recycle.

7. **Are there common spaces where students can grow vegetables or engage in other forms of permaculture?** Some people never had the opportunity to learn how to grow vegetables, but everyone should have a chance to learn how to grow fruits and vegetables without chemical fertilizers or synthetic pesticides. In the age of high priced buildings and tuitions, it's worth remembering good vegetable gardens can produce the food that preserves health and save families money. Creating a generation of young people that know how to grow their own food may sound mundane, but in our increasingly stressful and unstable world, getting back to the basics with food production is a good thing.

   One example of experimenting with permaculture at college is the work of *Wild Wes* (wildwes.blogspot.org) at Wesleyan University in Middletown, Connecticut. Working with the administration, students worked to convert an area of lawn into a combination of trees and flowers. It should also be noted that student clubs can experience a significant boost from the existence of the AASHE, as part of their role is to support "green" student clubs as they transition from year to year and in summers, which can be challenging for these student groups.

8. **Are the course offerings giving students the tools they need to win the Green Revolution?** We need college graduates that understand green energy from the perspective of all disciplines, including Economics, Environmental Science and Human Ecology. We can set goals and mandate green standards, but we need people with the knowledge to carry out these mandates and goals. The follow up question is; what should the average college

graduate understand about energy, nutrition and environmental policy? The more the better, but this is something colleges need to think about and answer well.

9. **Does the college investment portfolio include investments in renewable energy?** There are many American renewable energy companies that need investment capital — perhaps as important as *having* customers is picking the right companies in which to invest. The more colleges that invest in renewable energy companies as part of their portfolio, the more these companies will be able to grow and contribute green jobs and clean energy.

10. **Is there any connection between college science programs and renewable energy groups?** "Crop mobbing" is a good way to connect and contribute locally, other ways might be to participate in renewable energy fairs or farmer's markets. Another way is an internship. For example, George Mason University offers a minor in Renewable Energy, and students are required to complete an internship with a renewable energy group or company. In this way students acquire practical knowledge and the company or group they work for gets some needed help and fresh ideas. (6)

11. **Is the student body active in measuring soil quality, composting and waste?** Through our choices we are able to increase and decrease the value of our soil and water. This affects the water quality of our streams and air, greenhouse gases and sustainability of land productivity. (7) For that reason, any college with a science department active in measuring soil quality can be a real asset. One example of such an institution is the Cornell Waste Management Institute, which "provides training for students in multidisciplinary approaches to bringing university resources to bear on solving waste management problems." (8) The institute also offers short courses and workshops for government officials, waste industry people and the public. The question in my mind is: could students and professors in science departments of more colleges provide useful feedback on soil and air quality?

12. **Are there any innovation challenges for students to come up with solutions of their own?** Sometimes there is nothing like a little competition to get the blood flowing, especially for our college students. The RecycleMania Competition is one approach to green rivalries between colleges. Could this be expanded upon to other areas of green energy, on campus, such as coursework and green clubs?

13. **Is there any engagement between students and local "Safe Routes," "rail trail" or walking groups?** Like many other people in my area, spending time on "rail trails" has been a source of healthy, relaxing recreation. As a result, the dream of a network of connected trails throughout New England is something I think about every day. Members of the younger generation need to learn about these successful models, that they might be a resource in the communities they eventually settle in. The successes of rail trail and "Safe Routes" groups are not as well-known as they should be; profiling their work in the college classroom is one way to raise awareness.

14. **What are some good aspects of the Princeton Review breakdown and how could it be made better?** The Princeton review offers solid breakdowns on green campuses, although the ideas in this chapter are much more complete. That said, for students just looking to know if their knowledge is green or not, the *Princeton Review of Green Colleges* is just fine.

15. **Is there a solar water heater on campus and do students know how it works?** Solar water heaters are great money and energy savers, but choosing the right one requires some knowledge. There are active and passive solar water heater systems, solar panel water heaters and solar energy water heaters to choose from, and schools can help provide a little introduction to them in their class work.

    Widely used in China, Japan, Greece, Australia, Turkey, Israel and European Union countries, solar heaters still make up a tiny percentage of the market here in the states. (9) And, although passive systems easily gather energy in sunny states like California, colder climates require an active system, which likely necessitates a passive system with circulation pumps and controls. Currently, installation costs are high, however one fact almost anyone can agree on is that heating our water from the sun's power would take a great deal of power off the grid. All challenges and nay saying aside, colleges can help us greatly by teaching students how these systems work and by demonstrating just how much money and energy they can save. This can be a good first step toward greater use of the devices, which will in turn lower costs.

16. **How many students are familiar with wave energy?** One of the less explored approaches to green energy is the utilization of "wave energy," through which energy is captured from the surface motion of waves. According to one source, wave power

varies greatly by location, but apparently the coast of the northwestern United States is a "wave power rich" area. (10) American students learning about this increases the chances of someone successfully applying the technology down the line.

17. **Does the college utilize or promote electric and hybrid vehicles?** The transition to greater use of electric or hybrid cars may be a slow process, but resourceful universities can be a help in promoting the understanding of the vehicles. This can come through coursework on the inner workings of the vehicles, on-campus displays or even use. California State University at Monterrey Bay uses twenty electric scooters for parking enforcement and campus safety, which is one way to promote 'clean' vehicles on campus. Colleges can combine this with presentations on campus, "outdoor showroom style," something I'm sure the automakers would be happy to do and that students would enjoy. (11) In the case of California it should be noted that there are significant government incentives that other states may or may not be able to match, such as tax credits, rebates and access to the carpool lane. California State also installed two electric vehicle charging stations, a feature some colleges may not be able to afford.

18. **Do students understand the dangers of nuclear power?** The radiation leak in Japan in 2011 is the latest and clearest example of how nuclear power can go wrong. In my opinion, one problem is that most college graduates (or the rest of us) don't understand what went wrong or whether or not we're in danger of anything like that happening in the United States. With 441 nuclear power plants operating worldwide, this is something we need to work on. (12) For answers I looked to that northern gem, The College of the Atlantic. After all, this Maine college offers only one major — human ecology, defined as "The branch of ecology that considers the relations of individual persons and of human communities with their particular environment." (13) I assumed that if any college looked at the dangers of nuclear power they would. The college *does encourage students* to intern with a nuclear disarmament group in California, which is a great example for other colleges. However, I was unable to find any coursework that critically examined concerns about the safety of nuclear power plants. In fairness *they did have a lecturer* that talked about the subject, but no fixed coursework.

When I worked in security, I always felt; things were safe or OK until they weren't. For me it is the same with nuclear power plants; things are safe until they're not — in the case of Japan, until a tsunami hit the plant. My hope for the future is simple: that more colleges will teach us what we need to know about nuclear power to make informed decisions as consumers and citizens of the world.

19. **Is there a course that studies the current state of ocean fish populations?** In the words of the Pew Charitable Trust, "fishermen, conservationists and scientists have actively debated how best to manage our ocean fish populations for decades. But with so much at stake, it's critical that as many Americans as possible be actively engaged in this discussion." I couldn't agree more, but I've had little success in finding any colleges where courses on this subject were discussed. The minds of our college students can bring fresh new energy perspectives to the debate, and perhaps we can soon read about a college course that looks at these issues. One thing is for sure; if done right, this could be a win-win situation for fishermen, conservationists and scientists. (14)

20. **Are there courses that focus on reducing our dependence on foreign oil?** Reliance on foreign oil causes many problems, one of which is that when dealing with conflict in Middle Eastern countries we can't be completely objective because we need their oil. If we could become energy self-sufficient, then we just might be able to be leaders in any peace process. The question is; are there colleges that focus on how we can shake that dependence?

    There are a few possible angles that colleges could take in going about promoting a reduction in oil dependence. There is a lot of talk about the need for a national energy policy, but perhaps we can best reach our goals by working at the state level, for two reasons. Firstly, wind, sun and hydro resources vary a great deal from state to state. Second, we might do well to allow each of the fifty states to see what kind of plan they can come with. Just as our federalist system can be very useful in comparing health care delivery, so too might it be in the area of renewable energy. Perhaps a friendly spirit of competition between the states would allow us to compare the progress of different states. When doing their studies, students should have a look at the German model, a country that is on track to get fifty percent of their energy from renewable sources by 2050.

21. **Do students study the German energy model?** Wind energy accounts for a mere 1% of the electricity produced in the United States, although some believe we can get this number to 20% by 2030. (15) However, for a good model to follow we would do well to look at Germany's progress in renewable energy. After all, the amount of electricity produced from renewable energy has increased from 6.3 percent in 2000 to 25% in 2012. This is expected to continue to increase, and total renewable energy use should be at 30% by 2030, (15B) which is remarkable because Germany has very modest amounts of wind and solar resources. However, the enactment of the German Renewable Energy Act provided a major boost to the growth of renewable energy in the often rainy, not so windy country. The study of legislative acts like this could yield information and results we could apply here in the U.S.

22. **Do students learn about U.S. wildlife policy?** Most of us don't spend much time worrying about U.S. wildlife policy, but the decisions made every day have a significant impact on animal life. For example, wildlife officials kill about one million animals per year as part of "predator control" policy. (16) Why is this done and how does it impact animal populations? These are some of the questions that we need to be talking about. One aspect of this conversation is looking at the implications of the comeback of some animal species. For example, the bison on the Plains; will the rumbling herds not seen since the 1800's again inhabit our grasslands?

23. **Do students explore opportunities for expansion of the national park system?** Exploring the potential for expanding protected areas and national parks in the mid-west and east should be an area of great interest and focus. Striking is that the majority of the land reserves are in the south and mid-west. The problem is that with the growing population of our country, setting aside vast tracts of land becomes more and more difficult. This is especially true in the mid-west and east, where humans are numerous. (17) It should be said that many states without national parks have extensive *state* park systems, but we still should be looking for opportunities to protect our national treasures.

    One existing, successful effort to save some of our wild places is the effort to create "The American Serengeti" in the American Great Plains, which would be a giant step forward for American environmentalism. Currently, a number of groups are patching together a number of different tracts of land in an effort to recreate the wildlife-filled plains that Lewis and Clark discovered two hundred years ago. Student groups that learned about this could be a blessing to existing efforts by groups such as the American Plains Group. (18) It will be a great day for America when we can again enjoy the vast plains filled with wildlife, clean air and bright stars. The more this subject is studied on campuses, the better the chances are that we will realize the dream. A good movie on this subject is with Tom Selleck.

24. **Do students at New England Colleges learn about the proposed national park in Maine?** The proposed Maine North Woods national park is incredibly exciting; it would represent the first major new national park in the U.S. in a long time. More importantly, it represents a successful effort to preserve the environment and long-term well-being of those of us that love each of the four seasons in our beloved home region. As always, the question is exactly how college classrooms would engage such a topic. Questions in my mind include; could student support make the difference in making this project happen?

    For starters, I highly recommend that young people have a look at a video put out by the group, within which one woman does a fantastic job highlighting the need for the park. At a time when we are bombarded with images of decay, fear and war, it would be wonderful for members of the younger generation to take part in creating something awesome. Even better might be to link the discussion to supporting the *Veterans Conservation Corp.*, which places returning veterans in conservation jobs. Yet better might be for one or two of the twenty-five Northeastern students doing investigative journalism for Fox 25 to do a story on efforts to make the park happen. This would be an example of epic teamwork that could have epic positive results!

25. **Can students participate in local time banks through a school group or club?** The existence of a local time bank can facilitate the ability of our students to give and receive, including in the realm of green energy. However, the existence of a club on campus can help to make that connection between community and school closer. It also allows students to know other students active in the group. Students may prefer to do

exchanges on campus, and this group or club can give campus members a chance to get to know each other in their own environment.

Time banking is about making new friends and connections; through the TB students can get to know other green energy enthusiasts or students to share their passions with. Students can offer "green services" such as weeding, organic fertilizing, planting or just help harvesting. In return they can acquire knowledge or special skills they need.

The exchanges of time can involve the sharing of "green" knowledge such as guidance on how to build or maintain a vegetable garden more effectively. Or, science students from the college could do presentations on solar panels, solar water heaters, or anything else that could be applied to their future homes or existing homes of their parents.

26. **Are students connected with the goals of local Native American groups?** Many Native American groups are working hard toward great environmental goals, whether it is bringing back the bison to the Plains or becoming energy self-sufficient. The recent establishment of tribal colleges with green energy curriculum adds a whole new range of possibilities for reconnecting to naïve America tribes and their perspective. Ideally our colleges will be become aware of this resurgence and find common goals to work on together.

27. **Do graduates learn about colony collapse disorder?** Entire colonies of American bees have been dying in great numbers, all over the country. Studying the phenomenon known as "colony collapse disorder" could be of great use to the creatures that pollinate our flowers and much of the food we eat. Good movies that talk about this problem are on Netflix.

28. **Are there courses for learning about expanding our walking and bike path network?** Building and expanding upon existing walking and bike paths requires local people with extensive knowledge of engineering, politics and planning. The good news is that many colleges offer this kind of training already. Colleges with this coursework include the University of California – Berkeley, Portland State University, the University of Washington, the Harvard School of Public Health, West Virginia University, UCLA, Skidmore College, Texas State, Prescott College, the University of Oregon, Temple University, Augsburg College and the

University of Chicago. (19) As I see it, any community with a college in the area should look into having coursework on this subject that will create the "local experts" towns need to use every opportunity to build up the quality of walking and biking options.

29. **Do students learn about ways to deal with the large numbers of dogs being killed in shelters?** According to a show on PBS, the reason 3-4 million dogs are being killed in shelters every year is that breeders are producing too many animals, not enough are spayed and people tend not to go to shelters. According to PBS, the solution is to put restrictions on breeders, neuter cats and dogs from shelters, counter myths about shelters and place them in more attractive locations. (20)

    One college course that looked at the issue came from a unique perspective – the philosophy department. That's right; the University of Redlands philosophy course visited a number of shelters to look at ways to reduce the number kills. (21) One of the shelter's missions is to prevent animal cruelty and further educate and help people care for animals in a responsible way. How to deal with cancer in dogs, which has become a national epidemic, is a question for another day.

30. **Do journalism students at the college engage with local media?** Beginning in the spring of 2015, twenty-five investigative journalism students at Northeastern University began to work for Fox 25 Boston doing a series of investigative pieces. (22) For me, this was great news; I had long lamented the failures of the media to effectively deal with what I considered important issues. For me this was great news because I thought that perhaps these investigative journalists can provide the much needed enthusiasm necessary to support our struggling media. However, what we really need are for other colleges to do the same; if five or six of Massachusetts colleges would forge similar relationships with local media, perhaps this could provide our struggling country with the boost we need to get on a more positive, healthy and green trajectory.

. . .

Chapter Eight Questions

1. What are the four general advantages to better energy policy?
2. Does participating in a crop mob sound like fun to you? Would this be a fun event for campus clubs or groups?
3. How much of a difference could it make to the local economy if colleges committed to buying organic food from local farms?
4. What are some differences between organic and modern agricultural methods?
5. Do the colleges in your area work with local green energy groups?
6. What was your favorite question from the chapter?
7. Had you ever heard of wave energy before?
8. Have you seen and learned about electric and/or hybrid vehicles?
9. Do you think students are capable of working out solutions to some of the health or environmental issues discussed in this chapter?
10. Do you think time banks could facilitate the "Green Revolution" on campus?

9

A Healthier and Greener New England

"Most of the shadows of this life are caused by standing on one's own sunshine."

- *Ralph Waldo Emerson*

In this chapter we "bring it all home" by looking at the ideas discussed throughout the book and applying them to the quality of life in towns and cities of my home region of New England. It's exciting for me; every part of the region is so different but still there are steps forward we can take that are good for everyone.

Chapter 9 Concerns

A. RAIL TRAILS, PEDESTRIAN AND BIKE PATHS- Look at models of rail trails, bike and pedestrian paths in Massachusetts. We will consider how these paths can change our car-centric culture and help children relax in their learning environments.

B. EDUCATION- Look at a few examples of how themes in Education are being applied in Massachusetts. Those themes include the role of vocational education, teaching personal finance, walk-to-school programs and school lunches.

C. HOUSING AND HOMEOWNERSHIP- Look at a few approaches to housing in Massachusetts, including the role of variances, zoning, public transportation, shared ownership and timebanks.

D. HEALTH AND WELLNESS PROFILE- Encouraging trends in wellness as well as look at what role local colleges play in developing principles that we can apply.

E. MASSACHUSETTS MEDIA- Consider ways that the media can support themselves through taking an active role in writing about and profiling all of these issues.

. . .

Rail Trails, Pedestrian and Bike Paths

Like much of the United States, the social, cultural and architectural landscape of New England has largely evolved around cars. This is particularly true in rural areas and suburbs where most residents are obliged to commute to work or school by car alone. While cars are undeniably time efficient forms of transportation, they are limited in other ways. Cars do not provide more active, cost efficient or eco-friendly lifestyles—all of which are becoming increasingly desirable in our current economic and environmental climate. Children that are able to safely walk to school can reap considerable health benefits, but we have to provide the support and infrastructure through developing rail trails, walkways and bike paths throughout the region. The good news is that a number of Massachusetts communities are already participating in walk-to-school programs sponsored by Safe Routes, as well as applying the lessons of the Pedestrian, Bike and Information Center in their planning. (1) See the article I wrote in the Salem News in the End Notes for more about this.

History of the New England Railroad

Before the advent of the car a century ago, it was once said that "one could start at any hour from almost any town in New England and make the journey in an incredibly short time." (2) This was thanks to the vibrant rail system that had developed in New England during of the middle of nineteenth century. Over time, however, cars, buses and motorcycles gradually supplanted the role of the railroads. These tracks have literally remained untouched for more than half a century until the recent development of "rail trails," referring to the conversion of old railroad land into multi-use trails for activities such as walking, biking, jogging, and cross-country skiing.

Possible Uses of Old Railroad Land

The implications and possibilities of this trend are far-reaching for it follows that towns with old railroad land have a ready-available resource to convert into walkable green space. This space would also make connections to other towns, providing alternative routes to highways and main roads. For outdoor enthusiasts or community activists, maximizing these rail trails is a win-win venture. This doesn't negate the desirability of having pedestrian walkways or bike zones running throughout town and city centers; they are highly desirable but are usually costly compared to the return on investment for rail trails.

What are a few examples of Massachusetts rail trails that are a good example to follow?

The Danvers Rail trail is an excellent example of a trail that was built using only volunteers on existing land. The Mass. Central Rail Trail is a good example of great coordination between towns to create something that everyone can enjoy. After all, the trails connect twenty-four communities through one hundred and two miles of trails. Additionally, their website (masscentralrailtrail.org) point; that if the railroad is ever needed again it could be brought back. See the MBTA called the Central Mass. Commuter Rail Feasibility study (1996) for more information on that.

Education

In Chapter One we talked about five aspects of education: vocational programming, personal finance, physical education, language programs and artistic expression. Here we look at two of these themes at the state level; models in education that can help give young people the awesome life they deserve.

Utilizing Vocational Education

As is stated emphatically throughout the book, it is important that there be enough enrollment seats for prospective students in plumbing, electricity, carpentry or other areas in which students can acquire valuable skills. As recently as ten years ago, vocational schools were arguably underutilized, but with the economy going south in recent years, applications to vocational schools have spiked. An April 2012 article in the Salem News (Ma.) tells the story of the dramatic increase of interest in two local schools, where there simply aren't enough slots for the current number of applicants.

Table 9.2 Admissions in Two Massachusetts Vocational Schools (3)

	Applicants	Openings
North Shore Tech	380	125
Essex Agricultural and Technical Institute	500	130

Another point that bears repeating is the option for schools to implement a combination of traditional and vocational studies, an idea brought up in the report "The State of the American Dream." According to that report, not only would thirty to forty percent of students better suited for vocational programs, but as many as fifty percent would benefit from doing a combination of the two. At the time of the report (2001), these findings contrasted with the fact that only seven percent of students were enrolled in vocational programs.

What is an example of negative attitudes toward vocational education? My strongest firsthand experience of this brand of "educational snobbery" is a teacher at the Minuteman school in Lexington telling me about how her students at the vocational often feel negatively about being in such a program. Sadly, I've heard this story too often; I can't even count the number of stories I hear from people on the subject. This stories were frustrating for me to hear, because at the same time I was working in special education with young people, many of whom had lost all hope.

How can time banks interface with vocational education? A relatively unexplored option in most communities is the possible role of timebanks to provide opportunities for students such as training and employment. Ideally students in the trades can learn skills, earn time dollars and even receive guidance from local craftsmen. If a relationship with timebanks were properly developed, schools could help young people invest in their futures early on. As of April 2015, the only time bank I'm aware of that works with young people is the Merrimack Valley Time Exchange, part of the Coalition for a Better Acre in Lowell. That said, other timebanks might activate; as of 2015 Massachusetts communities with timebanks included Beverly, Cambridge, Salem, Northhampton, South Dartmouth and Lynn. (4)

What is the role of the local economy in education? One of the biggest issues facing young people is the lack of summer jobs, which prevents young people from getting valuable work experience, cash and references for future employment. However, one avenue to explore to create seasonal jobs on farms is to follow the four principles promoted in Chapter Four; Building Healthy Local Economies. Whether it's buying shares of community supported agriculture, or "CSAs", asking convenience stores to stock local produce, the continued expansion of farmer's markets or serving locally grown food in the schools, if people support local farms then that will create seasonal, local jobs for young people.

What is the the role of the ideas in Chapter Eight on healthy college campuses with regards to students in middle and high school? A shift in our culture from one obsessed with test taking to a culture that values healers, environmental leaders and educators will be great for young people for whom high school has often been a struggle. Exploring each of the concepts in Chapter Eight can create a college environment where all kinds of learners can thrive, including those who have a hard time with tests or struggle with anxiety. (see page 114) Why? Because a joyful, dynamic learning environment that takes an active role in building a brighter, more sustainable future is going to do better. Through doing graduate work at a Massachusetts public college, I can tell you the younger generation needs this, bad!

Physical Education: Standards and Needs

According to the *National Association for School Physical Education*, school age youth need at least 60 minutes of moderate-to-vigorous physical activity every day. Currently, Massachusetts and Vermont are the only New England states that require physical education at every grade level. However, that alone does not mean that the physical needs of the children in those states are being met. However, with the impact of state budget cuts, physical education programs often struggle to maintain their curriculums.

How does the system of waivers impact students in Massachusetts? In other states, the prevalence of waivers appears to be a systemic problem. According to the National Association for Sport and Physical Education (NASPE), thirty-two states offer waivers that allow students to substitute physical education for other subjects. (5) Within New England, Massachusetts and Vermont require physical education at every level, but waivers offer a way out, but of course the frequency and quality of physical education. Using physical education to improve the well-being of children is a subject that I hope future authors will seize and expand upon more than I have here.

What is an "outside the box" approach to the issue of young people not getting enough exercise? Promoting the Safe Routes models of children walking to school. The website of the national organization is filled with success stories of programs that led to a greater number of children walking to school and in so doing getting the exercise that they need. These walking programs can be combined with children get the exercise they need in school as well. You can check out the interactive website of Safe Routes to read about success stories in Arlington and other communities. (6)

What's a reason for hope in the realm of physical education that meets the needs of young people? I know from doing graduate work at one Massachusetts public college that there are countless students of physical education that would love to have a positive impact on the well-being of students. The doors of the professors and message boards of the physical education department are filled with (always rotating) articles that articulate the concept outlined in Chapter One; "that physical education teachers replace doctors as the great profession of the 21st century. To take the concept yet one step further, I hope that these physical education teacher will being to consider other awesome work being done in conservation in Massachusetts, work that will create the infrastructure and green space for people to enjoy and build their health. Whether we're creating walking and bike infrastructure or going for gold through the creation of a new national park in Maine, all of these positive steps, if responded to correctly, can support the well-being of the next generation.

Teaching Personal Finance

Although there was once a push in Massachusetts to teach personal finance in the schools, I worry that this effort is losing steam. (7) For that reason I choose to reiterate that to assure that students indeed learn the basics of mortgages, financing, renting, budgeting and credit we don't need to start new programs. Rather, we can integrate the instruction of this core survival knowledge into the school day in many ways, including as part of math class.

What is an example of a college in New England that teaches this personal finance? An example of this at the college level is Salem State University's financial literacy workshop known as SMART. Act Responsibly. Thrive. Taught by faculty of Economics department and the Bertolon School of Business, this workshop addresses how to make a financial plan, understand credit scores and borrowing, as well as containing core information about banking, saving and investing. The courses were highly popular and packed. In the words of one student, "I instantly fell in love with the idea because I consider it very important. In college, we learn the basics of math and history but when it comes down to the nitty-gritty stuff of wanting to function in the job, you need to learn that too." Unfortunately, this free program is rare; according to an article in it's only the second of its kind to be provided by a Massachusetts public college or university. (8)

How does this book advocate teaching personal finance? At the high school level as part of math class, although I was unable to find any examples of this. That's to say I'm sure that these programs exist; it's just that I was unable to locate them. I often emphasize that four hundred books could be written that explore these themes in greater depth; a book that compared different approaches to teaching personal finance in high schools could be incredibly useful and powerful.

Housing and Homeownership

The high cost of housing in New England makes, in this section we it challenging for young people to build a life and raise a family. For that reason we have a look here at a few perspectives and approaches to housing. Specifically, insights or approaches we can utilize to improve quality of life for everyone, especially those struggling in this economy.

Variances and Zoning

In Massachusetts, town governments have significant power, perhaps rooted in the old town meeting tradition. (9) This can mean tight restrictions on building permits. The reason for these restrictions is partially economic. In most Massachusetts communities, the cost of schools and other public services is very high. So if a modest house with low taxes is built, then the revenue for the town is low. For example, if that same house has five children, all of whom are in the public schools, then their presence could become a net financial loss for the town. City planners know this, and perhaps as a result communities often pass strict zoning laws that mean that many can't afford to build or buy a home.

One response to this was an idea put forward in the 2006 Massachusetts gubernatorial race, in which Kerry Healey suggested to provide tax incentives to towns that allow for adding accessory apartments that don't affect the overall footprint of the property. (10) That's one approach, but if we are going to deal with the growing issue of homelessness, we're going to need to look at all of the approaches to building healthy local economies outlined in Chapter Four.

Massachusetts Transportation Innovation

According to The Surface Transportation Policy's Project report Transportation Costs and the American Dream, transportation costs make up 19 percent of American household budgets. (11) So, finding affordable, accessible (and ideally healthy!) transportation within Massachusetts communities is very important economically. Alternatives to driving both mediate the high fuel cost of driving and allow individuals to take advantage of the lower costs of living in communities outside the city. At a time when our roads are congested and a cause of significant stress, investing a small amount in clean, safe ways to work makes sense. This book favors investigating multiple aspects of green infrastructure in multiple ways, seen below.

First, develop our system of walking and bike paths to give people healthy options for getting around. Chapter Three outlines approaches to this, including Safe Routes walk-to-school programs and principles promoted by the Pedestrian, Bike and Information Center.

Second, let's begin to dream of developing walking and biking lanes alongside Route 95/128, from south of Boston up to Maine. For safety there would need to be a divider between cars and the lanes, which of course would cost money.

Third, this book advocates all the steps outlined in Chapter Eight with regard to going green at universities. However, a good, easy way start is to utilize the handbook "Campus Sustainability Best Practices; a Resource for Colleges and Universities."

Fourth, communities need "local experts" that have done the coursework prescribed by the Pedestrian, Bike and Information Center. The Harvard School of Public Health used to offer the course on the budgeting, political and engineering aspects of building a long-term plan to be bike and walking friendly. See pedbikeinfo.org for more information on how walking and biking options are a boost to physical and mental health.

Shared Home Ownership in Rural New England

In all parts of New England it is increasingly difficult for young people to buy a home. I spent my winters in rural New Hampshire from 2001-2005 and noticed the spike in the price of land. I also heard stories about how the trailer parks that had been becoming less frequent were the only option that many young people could afford. One concept to respond to this for young and old (explored in Chapter Three) is the possibility of co-ownership. However, for this to become a viable option for younger people looking to acquire capital or older folks looking to downsize, lawyers need to work on coming up with better contracts that protect everyone from risk.

Although shared home ownership can be a good option for the vulnerable, especially veterans with PTSD, I like to emphasize the importance of exploring all of the ideas in Chapter Four; Building Healthy Local Economies to support quality of life throughout New England.

Table 9.1 Multiple Payers on a Mortgage

Size of Mortgage	1 Payer	2 Payers	3 Payers	4 Payers
$100,000	600	300	200	150
$200,000	1200	600	400	300
$300,000	1800	900	600	450

Note: The above numbers assume a 6% mortgage rate on a thirty-year loan. Any company that sought such a system would have to address a number of logistical and legal issues, and I recognize this.

According to one Vermont shared housing manager; "Shared housing provides a creative solution for people who, for a variety of reasons, choose to live in a mutually supportive environment. It is an alternative housing arrangement for many rural Vermonters who do not have access to affordable housing in their towns or who could not remain independent without a supportive environment." (11) Good news for Vermonters, but what about struggling folks in the rest of New England?

What needs to happen for this system to work elsewhere in New England? There is a lot of work to be done. Vermont may have examples of successful co-ownership but I spoke with a number of Massachusetts mortgage brokers about co-ownership and most had never even heard of such arrangements. Integrating instruction on shared ownership into personal finance classes at high schools and colleges is one way to share the knowledge.

How can lawyers help shared ownership help the needy? Lawyers can do the public a real service by beginning researching and developing models of shared ownership contracts, an essential aspect of making shared ownership work for those struggling to keep their heads above water. Whether it's recent high and college graduates looking to acquire capital, older folks looking to downsize or anyone else, there is a lot of work that needs to be done to make this work for people. If lots of good legal work is done I believe that this model might also work for returning veterans with no place to go, both from a financial and communal perspective.

Time Banking and Homeownership

Homeowners are often overwhelmed with maintenance costs, but through the timebank system owners can help others while and receiving essential services in return. There are many different time exchanges throughout New England successfully helping neighbors help each other. At the Onion River Exchange in Vermont, the Hour Exchange in Portland or the Cape Ann Timebank in Gloucester, time exchange organizations are helping make life easier for owners through the service exchanges and symbiotic relationships that timebanks help to create.

What are two groups that creative approaches to homeownership might help? Veterans and those struggling with opiate abuse. Many returning veterans suffer war-related trauma while over 1,000 people in Massachusetts died of opiate related abuse in 2014. (12) This is an obvious sign of a highly stressed society that needs to respond in every way it can, including through having a flexible housing market that offers options that can take the pressure off people. Whether we're looking to meet the needs of the disenfranchised, underprivileged, stressed, traumatized or just hard-working New Englanders, exploring how shared ownership might help is worth exploration.

Health and Wellness

Most of us in Massachusetts will remember well when Governor Mitt Romney, the state legislature and CEOs of major health care providers formed the famous state mandate that requires all state residents to have health insurance—a rule that made its way onto the national stage as the model for "Obamacare." (13) However, discussions of health should not be restricted to analyzing health care; we need to look at building the health of Massachusetts residents from a holistic perspective, including integrating the ideas on community in Chapter Four.

Causes of the Health Care Cost Increases

According to the 2011 New York Times World Almanac, nine causes of the increase in Health Care costs include; the use of sophisticated, expensive medical equipment, higher priced prescription drugs, arguably unnecessary procedures, and an increasing elderly population, an increasing number of accidents, and earnings growth for health care professionals, high costs of malpractice insurance, administrative waste and fraud. (14)

What is the best way to explore the ideas in the next section? We need the media to engage the public in debate. The problem is that print newspapers are understaffed and overwhelmed by the increasing complexity of the subject of health care. The good news is that investigative journalism in Massachusetts is getting a boost with the student journalists from Northeastern partnering with Fox 25 in the creation of multi-media stories. (15)

Four Models Worthy of Study

One of the advantages of our federalist system is the fact that we can compare the social service systems of different states to decide which one works best. However, studying a few models in Massachusetts (or over the border in Portland Me.) can be accomplished by a well staffed, dynamic media; both local papers with adequate community support and the new college journalists.

The health care clinic True North in Portland, ME is a model worthy of study because it accepts time dollars for payment and offers holistic treatment of ailments. Mass. Health is a need based public insurance model worth further study. (16) Also worth attention is the need for medical malpractice reform to lower costs and keep doctors in the state. (17) Third, allowing cities to save money by purchasing health coverage through the state is a model ripe for analysis. (18) Fourth, developing the tools for effective comparison shopping. (19) Catastrophic insurance can offer "lower-than-average premiums in exchange for higher-than-average deductibles," and is worth learning about. (20)

Existing Health Coursework on College Campuses

Above all I believe that the younger generation has to lead the way, and the best way is for college students to actively study all of these models. Below are three New England colleges that have some good coursework. I believe that an idealistic professor could do a great service by writing a book focusing on health course comparison, but for now you have four approaches here.

The Social Work Perspective (Massachusetts)

A good Social Science perspective of health care policy is offered through Salem State, "SWK 846." The course "adopts a social problem framework to examine and critically analyze health policies, health service delivery, and overall financing of health care in America." (21)

Any Social Work perspective should also consider the importance of education and learning about consumer options. With health care policies and packages changing so rapidly, one important point to be considered is our ability to effectively comparison shop; a point was made by the Healey/Hillman committee in the 2006 gubernatorial race.

The International Perspective (Massachusetts)

Taking place in Quito, Ecuador, a Boston College Office of International Programs offered an ambitious health care seminar; Nursing 345. The course description includes "an in depth study of global health policy from the perspective of various stakeholders: populations, governments, NGO's health care providers and health educators." (22) Students also will be evaluating "country specific" policies.

What approach is even more useful than the international comparisons? Country comparisons can be interesting and useful, but college programs should analyze the systems of the fifty different states. Analyzing different countries is good, but as a nation one of our greatest strengths is the ability to compare fifty very different systems in each of the states. The point of any such analysis is of course to learn more about what works well and what aspects need work, something the framers of our Constitution foresaw. (23) While the course in sunny Ecuador sounds great, I would emphasize the value of gritty analysis of the fifty different systems right here in the United States.

The Economics Perspective (Connecticut)

Just forty-five minutes from the Massachusetts border, the economics department at Wesleyan University in Connecticut takes a different approach, looking at the health care debate from the perspective of economics. The course description reads: "We examine the U.S. healthcare system in some detail, with some attention to useful international comparisons…other questions that we will address include: What is health? How is it measured and valued?" (24)

The approach of the independent-minded Wesleyan is closer in spirit to what I feel the country needs. However, they too might make the course even more useful by expanding from "international comparisons" to comparisons between the health care systems of the fifty states.

How might Wesleyan integrate the economics aspect of health with other dimensions of well-being? Extremely important to the success of any Green movement is to connect with others that struggle for the long-term well-being of the American people. The good news is that in the case of Wesleyan, they have the Wesleyan College of the Environment right on campus, a group whose mission is extremely ambitious; "to change the trajectory of the planet for the better." This may sound ambitious or even bombastic, but doing the research for this book has taught me that this is indeed possible.

• • •

Chapter Nine Summary

In her book the Silenced Majority, Amy Goodman wrote that "we need a media that covers grassroots movements, that seeks to understand and explain the complex forces that shape our society, media that empowers people to make sound decisions on the most vital issues of the day: war and peace, death and life." (25) This is especially true in Massachusetts, where residents desperately need new authors, college classrooms and local papers to explore and expand upon the ideas here.

What is a reason for hope for greater analysis of the ideas here by both universities and the media? In the case of Massachusetts we have reason to hope, due to the recent addition of twenty-five Northeastern journalism students to the ranks of investigative journalists, as part of a cooperative deal with Fox 25 Boston. Beginning in 2015, a number of high quality analyses by the investigative journalism students have already happened. (26) This is important, because the reality is that many of the local papers and understaffed and overwhelmed, which means that the kind of analysis the people need is just not getting done. However, this model, if imitated by other colleges in the state, could provide us with the kind of journalism we need to effectively respond to our ever changing world. Additional reason for hope; rumor has it that Boston University is considering a similar program.

Transportation and Green Infrastructure

Walking and bike paths in New England will give those struggling with physical and mental health the chance to get some fresh air and connect to their community. I wrote an article on how to make walking and bike paths happen in one Massachusetts town, that you can feel free to modify and send to your local newspaper, see the End Notes. (27).

Veterans Conservation Corps	We need analysis by our local papers and universities on how to support the Veterans Conservation Corp. in Massachusetts, which would both support returning veterans, conservation and the local economy.(28)
Community Reinvestment Act	Residents can consider paying greater attention to and supporting the funding that provides local aid to communities for maintenance and projects.
Rail Trail Models	**MassCentral Rail Trail at: masscentralrailtrail.org** **MassBike at: massbike.org** **The LaMoille Valley Rail Trail (Vermont) at: lvrt.org.**
Keeping Pets Safe	The ideas above can create the green space for animal owners to give pets needed exercise, keep them healthy and perhaps escape the cancer epidemic. The "no-kill" shelter model of the Northeast Animal Shelter throughout the state can save animals from the other great threat; euthanasia.

Education

The continued development of regional vocational schools in New England is going to be at the heart of any increase in opportunities and quality of life for young people. It's important to remember that there is more to supporting vocational education than building the edifice. It involves changing attitudes and confronting snobbery in many circles of Massachusetts toward the programs. I say that because I've experienced that attitude firsthand. I also know from talking to a teacher at Minuteman Tech that she thought many of the students felt almost a stigma from being in a technical school. In 2015, with young people and the world struggling, we need to celebrate and utilize our vocational schools.

Housing

While we may argue about what housing or zoning policies work best, I choose to focus on what most of us should be able to agree upon; teaching all young people the basics of mortgages, financing, renting and credit in school. When that happens in the Massachusetts schools I believe that people will be better equipped to make the right housing choices and not fall prey to predatory lending and credit.

Chapter Nine Questions

1. Are there any "rail trails" near your hometown? Have you been on one?

2. Is it exciting for you to imagine connecting the network of bike paths and rail trails into a New England network?

3. What is one way to build bike paths much more cost-effectively?

4. What do you think of the Safe Routes Brattleboro story? Could this model be imitated in rural Massachusetts?

5. Is table 9.4 helpful?

6. Do you think the "roommate pooling" model can help struggling young people?

7. Were any of the points on health care and wellness new or interesting?

8. Which "Health Care Course" do you like? Which would you take if you had the option?

9. What do you think of the idea that Massachusetts college classes study and ways to secure Social Security? Is this realistic or feasible?

10. What do you think are the best ways that the Massachusetts media can support public well-being?

10

Every Life Matters

"When written in Chinese, the word "crisis" is composed of two characters. One represents danger and the other represents opportunity."

– John F. Kennedy

The shooting of Michael Brown in Ferguson and the strangling death of Eric Garner brought out a great deal of anger that had previously only simmered below the surface. The mantra "black lives matter" that came out of the events was a great mantra and articulates a new, better attitude that I (and I'm sure many others) feel needs to pervade our culture. That mantra was turned in to "All Lives Matter" here, which is the essence of the spirit of this book; to improve quality of life for the black, Latin and white poor. At the same time, there is a focus on taking the pressure the off the police, because it they that have to bear the burden of bad policy. Yes, there is such thing as good policy that benefits *everyone.*

What is the format of this chapter? We start by looking at three "economic crises", each of which have contributed to the current unrest. The first is the massive debt and spending of the federal government, which threatens not only our economic stability, but with it Social Security, our best protection against elderly poverty. The second crisis is the mortgage crisis that began in 2007, leaving twelve million Americans owing more on their mortgage than the value of their homes. The third is the lack of full-time work opportunities for college graduates. First the crises, then we look at possible responses.

Chapter Ten Concerns

A. CRISIS ONE: OUT OF CONTROL FEDERAL DEBT AND DEFICITS-A better informed public through teachers and media.

B. CRISIS TWO: THE HOUSING BUBBLE-Is Shared housing the answer?

C. CRISIS THREE: FEWER JOBS, HIGHER COSTS-Do you know parents with adult children living in their basement?

D. RESPONDING TO ALL LIVES MATTER- 11 key factors addressing this fact!

. . .

Crisis One: Out of Control Federal Debt and Deficits

To reiterate the theme of Chapter Four, the wild spending habits of the federal government represent a real threat to the future of generations to come. The energy of the American people to secure Social Security is strong and could also be utilized to work toward more stable spending.

Table 10.1 Debt Predictions, 2010-2015 (in billions)

	Revenue	Spending	Deficit	Total Debt
2010	2,164	3,720	-1,555	14,456
2015	3,633	4,385	-759	19,863

What is the best way for the people to respond to out of control federal spending? We need the three approaches emphasized throughout this book; hundreds of new authors to write on the subject, well-staffed local papers that engage in analysis and a culture of problem-solving in classrooms on our college campuses through relevant coursework and projects. The class at the University of Georgia that came up with a proposed balanced budget (Chapter Five) is one example of the kind of work we need. I feel like I am in agreement with most Massachusetts residents when I say that it would help if local papers ask candidates for federal office to explain how they suggest assuring that Social Security remain solvent for the next fifteen, twenty-five and thirty years. Again, this is a theme that the Northeastern students working.

Crisis Two: The Housing Bubble

The mortgage crisis that began in August of 2007 has wreaked havoc on families and neighborhoods. Twelve million Americans owe more on their mortgage than their home is worth, which for many can spell the beginning of life struggling with debt. Combine this tough situation with other dark realities and we're in a situation where we need to be looking for answers.

Which book idea has the most potential to help people find affordable housing? One approach is shared ownership of housing, a concept explored in depth in Chapter Four. Through partial ownership, many can escape high rent by instead downsizing and paying a share of a mortgage. That said, there is a lot of work to be done by lawyers with contracts, zoning and education for this system to reduce risk.

Table 10.2, Shared Mortgage Payments (Approximate)

	1 Owner	2 Owners	3 Owners
$250,000	1,602	$801	$534

Note: This assumes 25% Property Tax & 0.5% PMI

What are the biggest challenges to this system working? First, there needs to be a good level of trust between the owners, which is hard because many people don't have anybody they trust enough to do something like this. **Note:** This is why lawyers need to work on coming up with better contracts for shared ownerships agreements, ones that address all contingencies, including zoning and parking issues.

Crisis Three: Fewer Jobs, Higher Costs

A recent study at the J. Heldrich Center for Workforce Development at Rutgers University found that "only 49% of graduates from the classes of 2009 to 2011 had found a job within a year of finishing school, compared to 73% for students who graduated in the three years prior. (1) The results of this study confirmed what many of us have been hearing all along from neighbors whose children still live in their basement.

Have you seen signs of the lack of jobs with your own eyes? Absolutely. I remember an Adolescent Psychology (great course, thank you Professor LaCroix!) course in the spring of 2013; out of the eight or so students twenty-five or under, all of them lived at home. Brutal housing and health care costs, combined with a lack of good paying jobs are prime suspects. In short, there is no one solution to this problem, which is the reason for the wide variety of steps forward offered here.

Responding to All Lives Matter

Low income Americans are the "symptom bearers" of many problems in New England. What that means is that they suffer the most from the shortcomings of the culture as a whole. For that reason, the successful exploration of the following fifteen ideas by new authors, college classrooms and local papers can benefit the poor the most. I for one hope this starts to happen as soon as possible.

One: Build Our Network of Walking and Bike Paths

Building up our network of walking and biking paths can boost our health and well-being, but the additional advantage is that they can help to integrate people of different races and economic backgrounds. Walking and biking on common paths is much different from sharing the same highway or freeway, which is why I advocate the many existing, successful models for us to learn from and imitate.

What are the three main approaches this book advocates? *Safe Routes* programs, rail trail models and the comprehensive approaches outlined on the website pedbike.org. The walk-to-school programs of the national group *Safe Routes* have had great successes; you can check out the interactive map on their web site to read about the success stories in your state. These ideas are explored in Chapter Four.

What are new approaches to creating walking paths? A third approach is to add pedestrian and bike lanes to existing while construction is already underway, as it cuts the bill from an average of $50,000 per mile to about $5,000. (2) However, for that to happen we really need local experts, which will happen through the more widespread study of coursework outlined by the group Walking Info. You can find and download the PDF for the proposed coursework for the Pedestrian, Bike and Information Center in the end notes of this book. (3)

How might this be particularly useful to the black community and policemen? The *Safe Routes* programs could help black children become more comfortable travelling in areas of the city or town where they otherwise might not be comfortable to go. The reverse is also true; people of all races can be comfortable travelling in different communities. Additionally, I believe that walking cities are healthier, safer cities, which makes the job of police easier.

Two: Secure Social Security

Many Americans are banking on Social Security for part of or all of their retirement. There is talk about reforming the Social Security system, but in Chapter Five I chose to focus on two realities of keeping the Social Security system solvent; transparency and containing health care costs.

Why is transparency important? Transparency of federal spending is of primary importance to the debate on Social Security because the federal government has to remain solvent for the system to continue to exist. The transparency and clarity that Citizen's Books and annual reports provide could help provide is a good start, although you should check out chapter Five to explore more on that.

Why controlling health care is costs so important for the elderly poor? People on fixed incomes are hit hard with the fifteen percent annual health care cost increases we saw in the 1990's and 2000's. They just can't handle a spike in the largest spending category, which is yet another reason to work hard to control health care costs. This is why we need to study how to utilize the federalist system by comparing and contrasting the fifty states and fifty different health care systems on college campuses in fifty states. A solvent Social Security system, combined with affordable health care, is essential to avoiding the misery of elderly poverty.

Three: Citizen's Handbooks & Annual Reports

Every person needs to understand his or her government, and nowhere is this more important than in a struggling democracy like the United States. However, things don't have to be this way. What if we could give everyone a user's manual for America? This is exactly what we can and should do by providing every American with a "Citizen's Handbook" that explains all aspects of government spending, complete with in-depth text and detailed graphics. We expect no less of—for example—corporate America, where shareholders automatically receive detailed reports on the company's dealings. In the same way, every American deserves a manual that provides the information he or she needs in order to truly understand our government and participate in civic life. (4)

Who should write these books? Just as some publishing companies make excellent profits by producing Alumni books for schools and colleges, a company could produce handbooks for states, cities, and towns. Owning a book that explains our state and federal government is especially important since the effectiveness of spending is important in dealing with unfolding crises. This could be a strong selling point!

What are existing tools of transparency that we can better utilize? One good, existing example of such a book is "A People's Guide to the Federal Budget," put out by the National Priorities Project. According to the group, the White House Office of Management and Budget released the last "Citizen's Guide" to the budget in February, 2001 to go with the 2002 budget request. (5) I dream of the day when town meeting members decide to expand their role and do this kind of analysis. The days of New England towns and villages isolated communities are over; to fight for quality of life, more Americans need to engage in this kind of analysis.

Who would we send these reports to? Ideally, these reports would be sent from legislators directly to the American people as an opportunity for legislators to share their hard work. Another existing model is that done by the *Mercatus Center* at George Mason University, including their "Annual Performance Report Scorecard of Federal Agencies."

What is another important principle of stability of our federal government? We should emphasize principles, not projections. One of the single best ways to keep federal spending under control is to insist on a balanced budget. Laws to this effect are already in place in several U.S. states, (6) but at the federal level it is generally referred to as "sequestration," a word which refers to "make the size of the Federal government's budget a matter of conscious choice rather than simply the arithmetical outcome of decentralized arithmetic process." Originally conceived in the Graham–Rudman–Hollings Deficit Reduction Act of 1985, (7) it was designed as a tool to reduce deficit spending.

Four: Engage Young Minds in Analysis

Chapter Eight talks about ways that our university campuses can lead the way in the "Green Revolution," whereas Chapters Nine look at a few ways our universities can lead in health and health care. Whether college classes focus on the format of annual reports or Citizen's Books, transparency isn't enough; we need groups of learners to actively engage in analysis and problem solving of our most pressing issues.

What are some examples of such useful college courses? One that could bring great rewards to communities is a course based on the syllabus put out by the group pedbikeinfo.org. The Pedestrian, Bike and Information Center created a mock syllabus that is designed to educate students on the budgeting, engineering and planning aspects of making a community more friendly to pedestrian and bike traffic. When communities have "local experts," or people that have done the coursework, then city planners can begin to construct ten or fifteen year plans for making the city a healthier place to be.

How could black Americans both benefit from and contribute to college campuses more engaged in problem solving and analysis? Each and every one of the questions raised in Chapter Eight; Winning the Green Revolution on College Campuses have the power to connect young, black Americans to the tools needed to connect the disenfranchised. We need fresh new energy to analyze federal spending to ensure the government remains functional enough to protect the vulnerable. Another

Five: Income Tax Simplification

"Keeping it simple" is a good approach in many areas of life, and federal tax policy is no exception. Anything we can to lower the stress of taxpayers and overwhelmed IRS agents should be considered. Second, making the system simpler can reduce cheating and fraud, which in the opinion of Steve Forbes is the single greatest cause of political corruption in Washington. (8) Third, federal tax code simplification makes it easier for the American people to understand tax policy, which gives us the clarity to better understand any future policy debates.

Six: Make Our Food Our Medicine

At a time when American waistlines, chronic illnesses and health care spending are expanding, more of us should consider the philosophy of Hippocrates, who said; "Let food be thy medicine and thy medicine be thy food." (9) At a time when many of our problems are food related, the tendency is to prescribe a pill instead of changing behaviors. However, one part of change could be to serve locally grown produce in the schools. Chapters Six, Seven and Eight profile ways we can work toward a healthier food culture. Doing so will give the poor and everyone else more of the nutrition they need to feel their best.

Seven: Create Semi-Public Bastions of Summer Fun

In my home region of New England there is a sharp dichotomy between the quality of summer recreational facilities available to the rich and to those that are not. A large number of highly expensive country clubs contrast with what are very small, often overcrowded pools. If you don't live on the ocean, there are few options for summer fun.

What is the model for this idea? German municipal pools. During my three years in that country I had little money but for the equivalent of three or four dollars I got use of a complex with three Olympic sized pools, including one for laps, one for diving and one for children. The shallowest of the pools even had a long slide, which was next to extensive green areas with volleyball courts and areas for Frisbee and soccer.

What are good locations for such facilities? Locations could be currently vacant properties for which cities are seeking alternate use. It's worth the effort to give everyone a nice place to go in the summer.

Eight: Maximize Education

All the education goals outlined in Chapter One can be of use to young people, which bear repeating here.

First, vocational education can give students marketable skills while offering other a more well-rounded education. For students coming from wealthy families this may not matter, but for those struggling to make it it's very important to acquire a skill.

Second, teaching personal finance is necessary to help young people understand how the world works; the most cost and time effective way to do this is to integrating it into math class. Combine giving young people a skill through vocational training with money management skills through teaching personal finance and we're getting somewhere. Again, students from wealthier families are more likely to acquire this knowledge in the home, but those coming from low-income comes are probably less likely to acquire this knowledge, even though they need it more.

Third, physical education and personal best programs can help students feel good and focus in their learning environment. The walk-to-school programs outlined in Chapter Three are yet another way to give young people the exercise they need to feel their best.

Fourth, art programs can help students grow, relax and connect with peers. Students need to look forward to the school day! Combine daily art with walking to school and daily gym and we are often adding to the quality of book learning time.

Fifth, we need to look at the practice of "tracking" and some issues it creates. Specifically, the tendency is to give struggling students busy work, which they too often alone. However, we are now learning that students need the exact opposite; lots of rich content, problem solving and work with peers. This is a practice that disproportionately affects children from low income families, which is all the more reason to change the system.

Sixth, we should look at the possibility of exempting some children from exams before they are ready. This opinion comes strictly from the experience of talking to a mother whose slow daughter went to high school every day but didn't get a diploma because she just couldn't pass the test. When I told her I was in favor of the MCAS, (a Massachusetts pass to graduate test) she yelled at me with tears in her eyes, which in hindsight I can understand. At the time of that incident I really didn't have any answer for her, but since I have seen enough of life to see why lifting the requirement of passing the test is fair to some. The point is this; if we utilize more creative approaches to building great school days for struggling children, from walk-to-school programs to quality physical education to great lunches, we can help give *all children* and not just the great test takers a chance to contribute and experience great joy and success.

Seventh, all of the goals of Chapter Eight can make a big difference to the value of the college experience. Put them together while we build our local economies and more will have a good shot at keeping their heads above water economically.

Eight, educate and prepare students in new ways to contribute to their families and communities. One angle for them to explore is ways to build their local economies, from good walking and bike paths to time banks to engaging with their local newspapers. In short, educate and enable young people in a positive way on the main points of Chapter Four. Some people may think that journalism and local print papers are a thing of the past, but I hope young people can come to see how much joy can come from local papers that report on healthy local economies that create healthy, happy, fulfilled people.

I also hope that children can take great joy in the preservation and expansion of our natural wonders. In the case of New England schoolchildren; *all of them* should derive joy in some way from the creation of the Maine North Woods National Park. Let them feel the joy and dividends will come back one hundred fold!

Nine: Let Our Colleges Lead the Green Revolution

We need better energy policies and some believe that a national energy policy is one way to address this. True or not, there are many advantages of reducing our dependence on fossil fuels. Myself, I choose to emphasize ways in which green energy can be addressed on college campuses, as outlined in Chapter Eight. However here we'll only the principal benefits of greater use of renewable energy.

First, greater use of renewables will allow us to invest the $300 billion that currently goes overseas every year for oil back into in the American economy. (11)

Second, the greater use of renewables will mean less pollution. Industry expert David Freeman argues that "the cleanest of the fossil fuels—natural gas plants—should be allowed to continue to generate power together with storage options, to assure reliability during hours when the renewables are not available." (11) However, any increase of our use in renewables (such as greater use of solar water heaters) can have an immediate impact in reducing our dependence on fossil fuels.

Third, since we will no longer need as much oil, we will finally be able to base our foreign policy in the Middle East on ethical principles instead of our energy needs. We won't need to worry about the instability of one Middle Eastern country because we won't need their oil.

Fourth, fixing our energy policy will result in our energy eventually becoming cheaper. Although much of the existing solar, wind, and hydrogen technology is expensive, with use those prices will come down.

Fifth, we must fix America's energy policy and come up with a reasonable way to power our nation because, in the end, we really have no choice. With world populations growing and multiple nations industrializing, the use of energy continues to rise sharply around the globe. If all of these countries continue to develop nuclear and fossil fuel options to power their newly technological lifestyles, then we will all be in for serious trouble down the road. The nuclear accident as the result of the tsunami in Japan is but one example of the many dire scenarios that await us in the future if we don't act now. Fixing our national—and global—energy policies to make them sustainable is a non-negotiable necessity.

Finally—and most importantly—we need to recognize that realizing the benefits above is only a small part of situations we are capable of improving if only we are willing to love and forgive each other, and then to work together, First we can move small stones together, tomorrow we can create a beautiful new national park system.

Ten: Engage Local Papers in Problem Solving

In my experience, many community papers in New England are struggling precisely as we desperately need informed, local voices that we can trust. A series of articles, reports, op-eds., round tables, etc., on subjects that affect us can reestablish the relevance of local journalism and engage the community in productive conversations. The rise of the Internet and the sharp decline of staffing, there was no one with the time to look at the crisis response ideas I was presenting. The worsening of our problems coincided with a decline in local papers, right as we needed them most.

What is a new area for local newspapers to expand into? One example is analysis of federal spending. What we have now is a situation where—to invoke a vivid and accurate image—America's relationship to the Federal government is like that of a parent to a reckless teenager who has been given all the credit cards and total control. Influenced by the writing of Thomas E. Woods, I've come to believe that it's also high time that we had a complete, top-to-bottom examination of American monetary policy and the Fed's role in our lives. Ideally, local papers would detail exactly how changes in federal policy will affect life in the towns the newspaper serves.

How can active local papers interfacing with college classrooms contribute to the well-being of people of color? They can help to influence better immigration policy. Talking about immigration policy shouldn't be about arguing about who is pro or anti immigrant; it should be about building good policy that will serve generations to come. I would love to see children from different countries in the Americas talk about their common dreams and share ideas. For example, the national park system is Costa Rica is one of the world's best; what can we in this country learn from their model? How can we work to protect our natural wonders together? These questions are only a few examples.

The Duke-Brookings Institute at Duke University held a roundtable in 2009, at which time people from all walks of life converged to study of immigration policy. It was an incredibly successful roundtable, one that offered a great number of suggestions as to how we could build an immigration policy that worked. They published their work "Breaking the Stalemate; From Deep Divisions to Constructive Solutions," which was the result of the work of hundreds of people. They did incredible work, but the work remains incredibly under utilized. In short, we need our colleges and media to raise the bar of the discussion and focus on the long-term well-being of everyone involved.

How might better immigration policy positively impact the health of policemen? I believe that thoughtful, generous immigration policies can help reduce some of the tensions and problems that arise when devoted policemen deal with hard-working immigrant communities.

Eleven: Keep Our Policemen Safe

Just as ideas in this book can be applied to help children feel better in their learning environment or help create employment locally, the ideas in this book can also be applied to keep our policemen safer. In fact, we can easily accomplish this if we "work together," as the late Boston Mayor Thomas Menino so often repeated. In fact, at the end of the day, the willingness to live those two words the late Mayor said so often are more important than any of the ideas here. I've done my job in creating this book; now it's up to citizens, new authors and college classrooms to come up with ideas of their own. It's all possible, if only we "work together." On that note, good luck in your quest to find what *you* can do to make our country a better place.

...

Chapter Ten Questions

1. Which idea in this chapter do you think is the best response to the current crisis?

2. What do you think about the potential benefits of "Citizen's Books" and annual government reports? Do you have any thoughts on their ideal format?

3. What are some existing models of approaches to transparency?

4. Can make the summer facilities model outlined here happen?

5. Do you think the proposed goal for world peace is an important part of this chapter? What do you think would be a good first step for its implementation?

6. What are four benefits of a national energy policy?

7. How can we work toward animals being treated with decency and respect?

8. Are there any other ideas from elsewhere in the book that belong here?

9. What is the role of community newspapers in the twenty-first century?

10. How are the walking paths and rail trails near you? How can the rail trail, Safe Routes or pedbikeinfo.org ideas be applied to your hometown?

|The End|

| Discussion Guide |

Although the book contains hundreds of ideas, all of them are united under one front; to improve quality of life for all living things. How to study these goals is up to you, but one thing is for sure; we're going to need many, many different voices to be heard for this work to have a chance to have a positive impact on people's lives.

You might ask what's the most important idea or principle of the book? Above all, we need to love and respect one other. The ideas in this book are great, but they mean little without our commitment to treating each other and those who can't defend themselves well.

What do we need; new authors, participation in college classrooms and Local Papers. It will take hundreds of writers to explore the relatively unexplored themes in this book. I believe there are easily enough themes here for hundreds of full books, if only folks take the time to find and develop them. College classrooms can contribute to the productive debate by doing problem solving and policy analysis in the classroom. The hearts and minds of college students can contribute to elevate the quality and spirit of analysis. Local newspapers can reestablish a new role for themselves by engaging in greater analysis; by helping readers understand how a rapidly changing world affects them. To achieve this, journalists will need a system to continue to develop their knowledge.

Below are 7 major categories you might want to discuss amongst yourselves after reading the book.

EDUCATION

Education can be useful in dealing with virtually every problem we have, from building health to green energy to creating joyful childhoods. These themes are explored in Chapter One and throughout the book.

1. **Vocational Utilization** According to the research of MassInc., as many as thirty to forty percent of high school students would be better off in vocational programs, with as many as fifty percent doing a combination of traditional and vocational studies. (1) How do we make sure that we create enough slots to insure that young people acquire the skills they need to survive?

2. **Teaching Personal Finance** Ensure high school students learn the basics of mortgages, finance, renting, credit and budgeting, ideally as

part of math class. Back in the 1960's and 70's when my Uncle Charlie was principal of Marblehead High School, talking to him about this would have been absurd, because everyone learned this stuff at home. Chapter Nine explores ways to impart this knowledge to high school and college students; what do you think is the best way to insure young people acquire this knowledge?

3. Daily Exercise How do we maximize physical education so children get the exercise they need to feel their best in their learning environment? Physical Education can then be synchronized with *Safe Routes* programs, "rail trails" and other approaches on the website www.pedbikeinfo.org (2) Another angle to explore is how these approaches can be integrated with steps forward in our environmental policy, such as the creation of new state and national parks. How might some children benefit from daily physical education, walking to school and being a part of the creative process of new national parks?

4. Model Language Programs Maximizing school language programs through more specific goals, better placement, books and other points outlined in Chapter One can make a positive difference in the lives of teachers, students and their families. How do we combine steps inside and outside the classroom (examples; physical education, healthy lunches and walk-to-school programs) to maximize student learning and well-being? How can college programs learn imitate existing, successful models at other universities to better their own?

5. Problem-Solving at Universities Tap into the energy of our college students to find solutions to challenges in health, energy and expansion of our national park system? Chapter Eight looks at thirty ways colleges can lead us to a brighter future, including through university/media partnerships like that created between Fox 25 Boston and Northeastern investigative journalism students.

6. Daily Art and Music Daily art and music classes help students to learn, grow, express themselves and look forward to school. How can we combine better school food and exercise to help students have great days at school? Can we make this happen at cash-strapped schools through creative approaches?

7. Healthy School Food Good people are working hard to serve healthy lunches in the schools, ones that help children feel their best in their learning environment. Models for this can be seen in the work of British chef Jamie Oliver and others; what do you think are the best ideas out there?

8. Special Education Can we combine all of the above ideas into approaches to create fun, productive, joy-filled days at school for those in special education? Can we improve upon the system of "tracking," whereby struggling students get the rich content, group projects and interaction with peers they need? Can this be done in an affordable way?

TRANSPARENCY, ANALYSIS & PROGRESS

1. Annual Reports How can existing reports on government spending, revenue and activities most effectively be shared with American households? Can legislators use these reports to share their hard work, whereas local newspapers can use them to see how constituents are affected?

2. Citizen's Books Might Americans better understand and support the good work of their government through "Citizen's Books"; works that analyze all aspects of spending, revenue and policy? This theme is explored in Chapters Six and Nine; what role do you think such books could play?

3. Student Engagement in Creating a Healthier Environment We need to engage the younger generation in proactive analysis of current policies. For example, should New England school children in science classes be learning about the value and role of the Maine North Woods Project? How can we connect such beautiful projects to the hearts and minds of school children that they might become stewards of our environmental treasures?

4. Community Newspapers How do we support local print newspapers and hard-working journalists? How might young writers assure their knowledge is enough to handle how complicated national issues affect locals? How might they interface with experts at local colleges? What is the process by which communities express their needs to their local papers? Is the Fox/Northeastern partnership a model for the future?

ENERGY & ENVIRONMENT

1. Renewable Energy How do we set goals to increase our use of energy from renewable sources such as the sun, wind and sea? Might a good first step be to look at education? What is the role of colleges and universities in working toward a future of safe and ethical energy production? These are some of the themes of Chapter Eight.

2. Expanding Our National Park System How do we engage universities, journalists and the public in building up our national park system? Are New England colleges engaged in supporting the creation of the new Maine North Woods National Park? How do we assure that *all Americans* can experience our natural wonders? Is the creation five proposed national parks in a Traveler's Magazine possible? Is this something for local papers to advocate for, thereby advocating access to these wonders for their readers?

HOUSING

1. Contracts for Shared Ownership Can we succeed in creating contracts for safe, low-risk shared home ownership? If contracts are improved, might recent college graduates, older people or veterans become possible candidates for this? Could shared housing arrangements (combined with securing Social Security – see Chapter Five) provide returning veterans with the structure they need?

2. Time banking for Homeowners Time banks can facilitate more comfortable home ownership through the exchange of services and productive relationships. How can time banks be utilized to give comfort and support to the elderly?

3. Solutions for Homelessness Shared housing and time banks are two concepts to for saving lives, but how might more dynamic local economies help the homeless? Ideas in Chapter Four explore answers to these questions.

JOYFUL, DYNAMIC COMMUNITIES

1. Community Pool Development Might the high quality semi-public summer recreation model outlined in Chapter Three work in some rural, suburban or even urban communities? Is exploring this idea yet another way for struggling print newspapers to rebuild their relevance? With thought and hard work, might young people have a fun place to recreate in the summer?

2. Participation in Preservation So many hunger to contribute to their communities, but how? Exploration of possible new national parks is one way to be a part of progress, but how can people participate locally? Is there a way for young people to be a part of new state parks? How do we protect our wild spaces and local farms? These are concepts explored in Chapter Eight.

3. Walking and Bike Paths Build and constantly improve the network of walking and bike paths through existing, successful models out there, including those of the national group *Safe Routes* and on the government sponsored website pedbikeinfo.org This is explored in Chapter Four.

MAXIMIZING PHYSICAL & MENTAL HEALTH

1. Explore the Core Education Points How can we utilize education to maximize our physical and mental health? What is the future role of physical education? How we give young girls the tools to systematically build their physical and mental health in the modern world? These are some of the concepts explored in Chapter One.

2. Winning the Green Revolution on College Campuses How can students and professors on college campuses lead the way toward a happier, healthier and environmentally friendly future? What role can they play in promoting the expansion of the national park system? Chapter Eight asks and answers some of these questions but it's up to readers to do a better job than I can.

3. Healthy Local Economies How can communities build local economies that offer opportunities for growth, comfortable living and employment? What role can they play in providing learning opportunities and employment for young people? These are the themes of Chapter Four.

4. Fitness for Older Americans How can we help the elderly feel their best? Is the most important principle that older people have someone to share and reach health goals with? These are the themes explored in Chapter Seven.

WORLD PEACE

1. Cost-Benefit Analyses Construct cost-benefit analyses of military and peaceful defense spending, including exploration of moving spending to programs such as the *Veterans Conservation Corp*, which provides returning veterans with employment in conservation projects. Instead of starting new wars we can employ veterans doing cathartic work that's great for everyone.

2. Food Self-Reliance Fear is the enemy of peace and one source of fear is food insecurity. Can the themes addressed in "Chapter Four; Building Healthy Economies" and "Chapter Eight; Winning the Green Revolution on College Campuses" help? Is permaculture a model for future security?

3. Secure Social Security Stabilizing federal spending on war could mean long-term stability for our government, which in turn could mean a chance for social security to be there for the younger generation. What role could college classrooms play in exploring how to make this happen? Might local papers find a way to engage community members on the subject? It's win/win.

Endnotes

Chapter One: Education

1. Edward Moscovitch, *Closing the Gap: Raising Skills to Raise Wages* (Boston: MassINC, 1997), Executive Summary, page 2.
2. Ibid.
3. Directed by Kristi Jacobson and Lori Silverbush, *A Place at the Table* was a 2013 movie that showed the plight of childhood hunger in America.
4. Education, *Washington Post*, http://www.washingtonpost.com/local/education/lunch-lady-rises-to-union-leader-and-takes-on-all-comers/2014/08/11/04895a82-1e46-11e4-ae54-0cfe1f974f8a_story.html .
5. Sum et al., New Skills for the New Economy.
6. Sheldon Berman et al., "The Rising Costs of Special Education in Massachusetts: Causes and Effects," in *Rethinking Special Education for a New Century*, ed. Chester G. Finn, Jr., Andrew J. Rotherham, and Charles R. Hokanson, Jr. (Washington, DC: Thomas B. Fordham Foundation and Progressive Policy Institute, 2001), PDF e-book, page 183.
7. *The University of Iowa*, undergraduate admissions, http://admissions.uiowa.edu/undergraduate/credit-exam-options Accessed: May 15, 2013.
8. People's Climate Summit Celsias, "South America Leading the Push toward Sustainability," *Clean Techies*, May 5, 2010 http://blog.cleantechies.com/2010/05/05/latin-america-pushes-sustainability/.
9. Sum et al.
10. Pomona College.
11. College of Liberal Arts Language Center, University of Minnesota, https://languagecenter.cla.umn.edu/tandem/.
12. Richard Brecht, "The Language Crisis in the War on Terror," The Eisenhower Institute, Gettysburg College, October 24, 2002, http://www.eisenhowerinstitute.org/events/past_events/old_events/102102Brecht.dot .
13. Dead Poets Society, directed by Peter Weir (1989; Burbank, CA: Walt Disney Video, 1998), DVD.
14. Ibid.
15. Jamie Oliver's Food Revolution, "Targeting School Food," http://www.jamieoliver.com/us/foundation/jamies-food-revolution/about_jamie_oliver.

16. Adolescent and School Health, Centers for Disease Control, http://www.cdc.gov/healthyyouth/physicalactivity/facts.htm.
17. This statistic was quoted on a March 2014 Edition of *Beat the Press*, a PBS roundtable style show hosted by Emily Rooney.
18. Guy Le Masurier and Charles B. Corbin, "Top Ten Reasons for Quality Physical Education," http://www.aahperd.org/naspe/publications/teachingtools/upload/top10reasonsforqualitype.pdf, May 14, 2013.
19. Corbin and Le Masurier.
20. Catelli, Linda A., Failing at Fairness; How America's Schools Cheat Girls, "Bottom of the Ninth; Girls Physical Education and Literature".
21. Jamie Oliver's Food Revolution http://www.jamieoliver.com/us/foundation/jamies-food-revolution/about_jamie_oliver.
22. Ibid.
23. Puneet Killipara, "Government still trying to catch up on foreign language capabilities," *The Hill*, June 12, 2010, http://thehill.com/homenews/senate/102833-government-still-trying-to-catch-up-on-foreign-language-capabilities.
24. Colorado State Gisela B. Estes, Barbara Lopez-Mayhew, Marie Therese Gardner, "Writing in the Foreign Languages Department," August 1998, http://wac.colostate.edu/journal/vol9/estes.pdf.
25. "Technology Brings Spanish Playrights into the Classroom," The College of Wooster News and Events, Feb. 27, 2013. www.wooster.edu/news/releases/2013/february/spanish-311.
26. LaFranchi, Howard, "U.S. No Longer Towers Over Latin America," http://www.csmonitor.com/USA/Foreign-Policy/2009/0418/p02s04-usfp.html.
27. College of Liberal Arts Language Center, University of Minnesota, https://languagecenter.cla.umn.edu/tandem/.
28. Andy Sum et al., *New Skills for the New Economy* (Boston: MassINC, 2000), http://www.massinc.org/Research/New-Skills-for-a-New-Economy.aspx.
29. Richard Brecht, *The Eisenhower Institute at Gettysburg College.*
30. Richard Brecht.
31. Dead Poets Society, directed by Peter Weir (1989; Burbank, CA: Walt Disney Video, 1998), DVD.
32. *New Skills for the New Economy* (MassInc.).
33. *The University of Iowa*, undergraduate admissions, http://admissions.uiowa.edu/undergraduate/credit-exam-options Accessed: May 15, 2013.
34. Wesleyan University is a liberal arts college in Middletown, Connecticut with high academic standards and a serious emphasis on public service.
35. Joseph T. Scarry, "Big Brother in Area Studies," *The Harvard Crimson*, December 5, 2003, http://www.thecrimson.com/article/2003/12/5/big-brother-in-area-studies-with/.
36. Scarry, Joseph T.
37. Colorado St. Gisela B. Estes, Barbara Lopez-Mayhew, Marie Therese

Gardner, "Writing in the Foreign Languages Department," August 1998, http://wac.colostate.edu/journal/vol9/estes.pdf.

38. Technology Brings Spanish Playrights into the Classroom," The College of Wooster News and Events, Feb. 27, 2013.

39. University of Minnesota TandemPlus.

40. Reed College Residence Life www.reed.edu/res life/on campus/language houses.html

41. University of Indiana.

42. Wesleyan University German House.

43. University of Iowa.

44. *L.A. Times*, http://www.latimes.com/opinion/op-ed/la-oe-allen-adjunct-professors-20131222-story.html.

45. Audrey Williams June, "How Universities Treat Adjuncts Limits Their Effectiveness in the Classroom, Report Says", *The Chronicle for Higher Education* http://chronicle.com/article/Adjuncts-Working-Conditions/133918/.

46. Ibid.

47. Ibid.

48. Sheldon Berman.

49. Making Every Village a University.

50. *The University of Iowa*, undergraduate admissions, http://admissions.uiowa.edu/undergraduate/credit-exam-options Accessed: May 15, 2013.

51. Sum et al., *New Skills for the New Economy.*

52. Albert Shanker, United Federation of Teachers, http://www.uft.org/who-we-are/history/albert-shanker.

Chapter Two: Keeping the American Dream Alive

1. Mark Erlich, "About MassINC," *MassInc*, accessed June 7, 2012, http://www.massinc.org/About/Voices/Mark-Erlich2.aspx.

2. "How it Works," *Cape Ann Time bank*, accessed December 1, 2011, http://www.capeanntimebanks.org/How_it_Works.html.

3. *Wikipedia*, s.v. "Time banking," accessed January 20, 2012, http://en.wikipedia.org/wiki/Time_banking.

4. Ibid.

5. Andy Sum et al., *The State of the American Dream in Massachusetts, 2002* (Boston: MassINC, 2002), 133, 117, 119, 118, 132, http://www.massinc.org/Research/The-State-of-the-American-Dream.aspx.

6. Ibid., 110.

7. "What It Costs to Go to College," *CollegeBoard*, accessed December 27, 2011, http://www.collegeboard.com/student/pay/add-it-up/4494.

html.

8. "Sticker Price vs. Affordability," *CollegeBoard*, accessed December 27, 2011, http://www.collegeboard.com/student/pay/add-it-up/4494.html.
9. Anna Maria Andriotis, "6 Colleges Cutting Tuition," *Yahoo! Finance*, February 10, 2012, http://finance.yahoo.com/news/6-colleges-cutting-tuition.html.
10. New York Times, page 327, "Number of Inmates under Jurisdiction of State or Federal Correctional Authorities, Year End 2000, 2008 and 2009".
11. Neighborhood Reinvestment Corporation, 2002 Homebuyer Education Methods Course Manual.
12. Robert Dietz, "The Social Consequences of Home Ownership," Ohio State University Department of Economics and Center for Urban and Regional Analysis, 2003, accessed February 20, 2012, http://web.mit.edu/~cwuz/Public/14.33/dietz%20social_consequences.PDF.
13. "Anxiety statistics," *anxietycentre.com*, accessed June 7, 2012, http://www.anxietycentre.com/anxiety-statistics-information.shtml.
14. Kevin Drum, "Poverty and Stress," *Mother Jones*, April 5, 2009, http://motherjones.com/kevin-drum/2009/04/poverty-and-stress.
15. Sum et al., *The State of the American Dream in Massachusetts*, 119.
16. Ibid., 117.
17. Ibid., 119.
18. Ibid., 118.
19. Ibid., 132.
20. "What it Costs to Go to College."
21. New York Times, page 327, "Number of Inmate under Jurisdiction of State or Federal Correctional Authorities, Year End 2000, 2008 and 2009".
22. "Go Out and Play!" *The Cornell Lab of Ornithology*, accessed June 7, 2012, http://www.birds.cornell.edu/celebration/temporary/go-outside-and-play.
23. In recent interviews, many young people cited a lack of a healthy relationship with adults as part of the problem. "Only 41% of dropouts reported having someone to talk to about personal problems. 62% said they would like to see schools do more to help students with problems outside of class. Only 47% said the schools even bothered to contact them after they dropped out." See "Dropout Prevention," *Solutions for America*, accessed June 7, 2012, http://www.solutionsforamerica.org/healthyfam/dropout_prevention.htm.

24. Wikipedia, s.v. "Time banking," accessed January 22, 2012.
25. Sum et al., *The State of the American Dream in Massachusetts*, 135.
26. Ibid., 122, 124.
27. Ibid., 103.
28. Ibid., 135, 138.
29. "Cancer Strategy #1: Low Oxygen Levels Breed Cancer," *Cancer Fighting Strategies*, accessed February 20, 2012, http://www.cancerfightingstrategies.com/oxygenation.html.
30. Ibid.
31. Sum et al., *The State of the American Dream in Massachusetts*, 119.
32. Ibid., 135, 138.
33. John C. Wright, ed., *The New York Times Almanac 2011: The Almanac of Record* (New York: Penguin, 2010), 381.
34. "Education Facts at a Glance," *Infoplease*, accessed June 7, 2012, http://www.infoplease.com/spot/schoolfacts1.html#ixzz1juzncCcv.
35. Amy Zimmer, "High-Priced Neighborhoods Less Safe for Property Crime, Report Says," *DNAinfo.com*, last modified September 27, 2011, http://www.dnainfo.com/20110927/upper-east-side/east-west-harlem-safer-for-property-crime-than-ues-soho#ixzz1jvT8qsxU.
36. *The Rushey Green Exchange Times*, January 2011, http://www.rgtb.org.uk/Newsletters/january_11.pdf.
37. Sum et al., *The State of the American Dream in Massachusetts*, 135.
38. Ibid., 117.
39. Ibid., 135.
40. Ibid., 131.
41. Wright, 304, 381-3.
42. Ibid., 381.
43. Ibid.

Chapter Three: Creating Opportunities for the Common Man

1. *The New York Times Almanac 2011*, 381-3.

2. From a speech before the American Society of Newspaper Editors, April 16, 1953. See Robert Schlesinger, "The Origins of That Eisenhower 'Every Gun That Is Made...' Quote," *U.S. News & World Report*, September 30, 2011, http://www.usnews.com/opinion/blogs/robert-schlesinger/2011/09/30/the-origins-of-that-eisenhower-every-gun-that-is-made-quote.

2. Bridget Terry Long, Dana Ansel, and Greg Leiserson, *Paying for College: The Rising Cost of Higher Education* (Boston: MassINC, 2006), http://www.massinc.org/Research/Paying-for-College.aspx.

3. "Case Studies", Pedestrian, Bike and Information Center http://

www.pedbikeinfo.org/data/casestudies.cfm.

4. Ibid.
5. Ibid.
6. Home costs.
7. "Fox 25 News partners with Northeastern University's School of journalism", http://www.northeastern.edu/camd/journalism/2015/01/21/fox25-news-partners-northeastern-universitys-school-journalism/.
8. Wright, *The New York Times Almanac 2011*, 381-3.
9. Northeastern School of Journalism.
10. True North "About Us," *True North*, accessed June 7, 2012, http://www.truenorthhealthcenter.org/about.asp.
11. UNH. http://www.huffingtonpost.com/2012/08/15/cost-of-college-degree-increase-12-fold-1120-percent-bloomberg_n_1783700.html.
12. Andriotis, "6 Colleges Cutting Tuition."
13. "Big Future" by *The College Board*, https://bigfuture.collegeboard.org/sitesearch?searchType=bf_site&tp=bf&q=two+year+colleges Accessed August 23, 2014.
14. Gerald T. Carey, "Social Security benefit increase no windfall," *The Salem News*, December 26, 2011, http://www.salemnews.com/opinion/x191079721/Letter-Social-Security-benefit-increase-no-windfall.
15. James D. Agresti and Stephen F. Cardone, "Social Security Facts," *Just Facts*, last modified February 20, 2012, http://www.justfacts.com/socialsecurity.asp.

Chapter Four: Building Healthy Economies

1. The full quote being referred to is from chapter three of Henry David Thoreau's *Walden*, titled "Reading": "It is time that villages were universities....If we live in the Nineteenth Century, why should we not enjoy the advantages which the Nineteenth Century offers? Why should our life be in any respect provincial?" Thoreau was a 19th century Massachusetts poet and member of the Transcendentalists, a philosophical movement that developed in the 1830s and 1840s in New England as a protest to the general state of culture and society, and in particular, the state of intellectualism at Harvard University.

2. "History of the Railroad in Danvers," *Danvers Rail Trail*, accessed February 4, 2011, http://www.danversrailtrail.org/history.htm.

3. Ibid.

4. "Bicycle Lanes," *Walkinginfo.org*, accessed January 26, 2012, http://www.walkinginfo.org/engineering/roadway-bicycle.cfm.

5. The chart and the monthly payments assume a 6% interest rate on a 30 year mortgage loan. Taxes and fees were not factored into the charts.
6. "Mortgage Default: What happens if I am a co-borrower and one of us defaults?" *PodProperty*, accessed January 26, 2012, http://www.podproperty.com.au/faqs.php#18.
7. See the website for the Arts & Business Council of Greater Boston: http://www.artsandbusinesscouncil.org.
8. This statement is based upon research found in MassINC's *The State of the American Dream, 2002*. Table 2.2 in Chapter Two of the report shows the relationship between educational attainment and income, and one can clearly see the declining incomes of those who have only a high school education.
9. See Thoreau's "Reading" chapter again.
10. Dr. Edgar S. Cahn is the creator of Time Dollars and the founder of Time Banks USA as well as the co-founder of the National Legal Services Program and the Antioch School of Law (now the David A. Clarke School of Law). Among many other works, he is the author of "Time Dollars" (co-author Jonathan Rowe, Rodale Press, 1992) and "Hunger USA." See http://time banks.org/about/board-of-directors.
11. See "The big idea" at Rushey Breen Time Bank, http://www.idea.gov.uk/idk/core/page.do?pageId=30211720.
12. "Digital Media and Learning Fact Sheet," *MacArthur Foundation*, accessed June 7, 2012, http://digitallearning.macfound.org/atf/cf/%7B7E45C7E0-A3E0-4B89-AC9C-E807E1B0AE4E%7D/DL%20FACT%20SHEET.PDF.
13. Christianna Reinhardt, "Food Jobs: Arroyo Time bank," *KCET*, December 15, 2011, http://www.kcet.org/socal/food/the-nosh/food-jobs-arroyo-time-bank.html.

Chapter Five: Securing and Maximizing Social Security

1. http://www.usfederalbudget.us/welfare_budget_2012_4.html
2. Wright, The New York Times Almanac 2011, 162.
3. "Federal Budget 101: Why Should You Care about the Federal Budget?" National Priorities Project, accessed June 7, 2012, http://nationalpriorities.org/budget-basics/federal-budget-101/?redirected=true#spending.
4. John C. Wright, ed., The New York Times Almanac 2007: The Almanac of Record (New York: Penguin, 2006), 162.
5. U.S. Government Printing Office, Budget of the United States Government, Fiscal Year 2002, accessed June 7, 2012, http://www.gpo.gov/fdsys/browse/collection.action?collectionCode=BUDGET&browsePath=Fiscal+Year+2002&isCollapsed=false&leafLevelBrowse=false&isDocumentResults=true&ycord=0.
6. Wright, The New York Times Almanac 2007, 163.
7. U.S. Government Printing Office, Budget of the United States Government, Fiscal Year 2002.

8. Ibid.
9. Medicare and Medicaid, http://www.encyclopedia.com/topic/Medicare_and_Medicaid.aspx
10. Ibid.
11. Ibid.
12. Congressional Budget Office, "Federal Debt and Interest Costs," December 14, 2010, http://www.cbo.gov/publication/21960.
13. Office of Management and Budget, historical Tables, http://www.whitehouse.gov/omb/budget/Historicals
14. United States Census Bureau, Bicentennial Edition; Historical Statistics of the United States, Colonial Times to 1970 (Washington, DC: 1975), http://www2.census.gov/prod2/statcomp/documents/CT1970p1-01.pdf.
15. Wright, The New York Times Almanac 2011, 162.
16. U.S. Office of Management and Budget, Fiscal Year 2012 Historical Tables: Budget of the U.S. Government (Washington, DC: Government Printing Office, 2010), http://www.whitehouse.gov/sites/default/files/omb/budget/fy2012/assets/hist.pdf.
17. Wright, The New York Times Almanac 2011, 159.
18. Ibid.
19. Ibid.
20. "Federal Budget 101."
21. Agresti and Cardone, "Social Security Facts."
22. Ibid
23. Media Nation, http://dankennedy.net/2015/01/23/northeasterns-journalism-school-to-partner-with-fox-25/

Chapter Six: Simplifying the Federal Tax System

1. This quote is courtesy of a story on the PBS website titled "Summary of Steve Forbes' Flat Tax Plan," *PBS Newshour*, accessed February 2, 2012, http://www.pbs.org/newshour/bb/congress/forbes_flat_tax.html.
2. Ibid.
3. "Who Pays Income Taxes?" *National Taxpayers Union*, accessed June 7, 2012, http://ntu.org/tax-basics/who-pays-income-taxes.html.
4. Ibid.
5. Maine Woods National Park Project, http://www.mainewoodsnationalpark.com/the-park.html.
6. Traveler's Five Picks for New National Parks, http://www.nationalparkstraveler.com/2013/07/travelers-five-picks-new-national-parks23553.
7. Sequence Inc. is a firm that has completed hundreds of forensic accounting engagements. They write, "Core competencies

include fraud examinations related to embezzlement, financial statement fraud, investment fraud, Ponzi schemes, SEC inquiries and investigations, and white collar criminal defense." Their blog includes commentary on issues potentially relevant to their work, including tax law. The quote above comes from one of their blogs: Brian Mahany, "IRS overwhelmed by New Tax Law Changes" *The Fraud Files*, accessed November 29, 2011, http://www.sequenceinc.com/fraudfiles/2011/09/irs-overwhelmed-by-new-tax-law-changes.

8. David Storobin, "The Flat Tax Revolution in Europe," *Global Politician*, May 8, 2006, http://www.globalpolitician.com/22020-europe.
9. Ibid.
10. "Summary of Steve Forbes' Flat Tax Plan."
11. Catherine Rampbell, "How Much Americans Actually Pay in Taxes," *Economix*, *The New York Times*, April 8, 2009, http://economix.blogs.nytimes.com/2009/04/08/how-much-americans-actually-pay-in-taxes.

Chapter Seven: Building Health and Well-Being

1. *The Rushey Green Exchange Times*, January 2011, http://www.rgtb.org.uk/Newsletters/january_11.pdf.
2. Anxiety Centre, http://www.anxietycentre.com/anxiety-statistics-information.shtml.
3. Ibid.
4. A Call to Revolutionize Chronic Pain Care in America, May Day Report http://maydaypainreport.org/.
5. The Kim Foundation, Mental Disorders in America, http://www.thekimfoundation.org/html/about_mental_ill/statistics.html.
6. "Impact of Stress," pdf, *American Psychological Association.*
7. Suicide Among Adults 35-64 Years, Centers for Disease Control, http://www.cdc.gov/mmwr/preview/mmwrhtml/mm6217a1.htm.
8. *The Rushey Green Exchange Times*, January 2011 *The American Senior Fitness Association*, Vital, Senior Specific, Fitness Education Made Easy for Colleges and Universities, http://www.seniorfitness.net/college_details.htm.
9. Elizabeth Quinn, About.com, "Many Seniors Lose Fitness Due to Lack of Training, Not Just Aging, May 12, 2011.
10. Ibid.
11. "Psychosis and the Elderly Person," *Mental Health Forum*, http://www.mentalhealthforum.net/conditions-and-experiences/psychosis-and-the-elderly-person/.

12. *The Rushey Green Exchange Times*, January 2011.

13. Senior Fitness Training, Professional Certificate Program, Western Carolina University, http://wcu.edu/academics/edoutreach/conted/profdev/nutrition-fitness-health-online-certificate-programs/senior-fitness-training.asp.

14. CSA also refers to a particular network or association of individuals who have pledged to support one or more local farms, with growers and consumers sharing the risks and benefits of food production. Courtesy of *Wikipedia.*

15. North Livingston Rv, http://www.northshorerv.com/html/indian_reservation.html.

16. *Rushey Green Times.*

17. Ibid.

18. "Osteoporosis," The Mayo Clinic, December 13, 2011, http://www.mayoclinic.com/health/osteoporosis/DS00128.

19. Holcomb. B. Noble, "A Secret of Health in Old Age; Muscles," The New York Times, October 20, 1998, http://www.nytimes.com/1998/10/20/science/a-secret-of-health-in-old-age-muscles.html?pagewanted=all&src=pm.

20. Fraser, Matthew J. "Making Walker and Bike Paths Friendly," *Salem News*, August 21, 2014, page 11. http://www.salemnews.com/opinion/letters_to_the_editor/article_d755f350-28fd-11e4-8fab-001a4bcf887a.htm.

21. Stephanie Watson, "Amazing Facts about Heart Health and Heart Disease," WebMD, accessed February 27, 2012, http://www.webmd.com/heart/features/amazing-facts-about-heart-health-and-heart-disease.

22. Elizabeth Quinn, About.com, "Many Seniors Lose Fitness Due to Lack of Training, Not Just Aging, May 12, 2011.

23. Working the mind and Alzheimer's.

24. "Flexibility and Coordination Exercise", HomeFitnessEssentials.com, http://www.homefitnessessentials.com/flex.php.

25. Shirley Archer, "Tai Chi Reduces Fear of Falling in Older Adults," IDEA Health & Fitness Association, January 2006, http://www.ideafit.com/fitness-library/tai-chi-reduces-fear-falling-older-adults.

26. Ibid.

27. Charlene Laino, "Resistance Training Improves Flexibility, Too," *WebMd*, Fitness and Exercise, http://www.webmd.com/fitness-exercise/news/20100604/resistance-training-improves-flexibility-too.

28. Senior Fitness Training, Western Carolina University.

29. Shirley Archer, "Deep Breathing and Pain Management," IDEA Health & Fitness Association, November 2006, http://www.ideafit.com/fitness-library/deep-breathing-and-pain-management.

30. "Frequently Asked Questions," TheWalkingSite.com, http://www.thewalkkinsite.com/faq.html.

31. "Strength Training," The Walking Site, accessed February 27, 2012, http://www.thewalkingsite.com/strength.html.

32. *True North Health Clinic.*

33. "Physical Health," Time banking UK, accessed February 27, 2012, http://www.time banking.org/about/timebanking-resources/research/physical-health.

34. See Chapter Three, Note 1 for more about Transcendentalism. By definition, "Transcendentalism is a philosophical movement that developed in the 1830's and 1840's in the New England region of the United States as a protest to the general state of culture and society, and in particular, the state of intellectualism at Harvard University and the doctrine of the Unitarian church taught at Harvard Divinity School. Among the transcendentalists' core beliefs was the inherent goodness of both man and nature. Transcendentalists believed that society and its institutions - particularly organized religion and political parties - ultimately corrupted the purity of the individual. They had faith that man is at his best when truly "self-reliant" and independent. It is only from such real individuals that true community could be formed." See Wikipedia, s.v. "Transcendentalism," http://en.wikipedia.org/wiki/Transcendentalism.

35. Food Matters, 2008, Carlo Ledesma.3

6. Forks Over Knives, 2011, Lee Fulkerson.

37. "How do You Know When testosterone Levels are too Low?" WebMd., http://www.webmd.com/men/features/low-testosterone-explained-how-do-you-know-when-levels-are-too-low.

38. "Anxiety and Panic Disorders", Southern California Center for Anti-Agin, http://socalbhrt.com/anxiety-and-panic-disorders/.

39. "The Story of Silent Spring," http://www.nrdc.org/health/pesticides/hcarson.asp.

40. Hippocratic Oath, Indiana University, http://www.indiana.edu/~ancmed/oath.htm.

41. Fraser, Matthew J. "Making Walker and Bike Paths Friendly," *Salem News*, August 21, 2014, page 11.

Chapter Eight: Building Peace and Progress on College Campuses

1. Jon Huntsman, "Energy Policy" (speech, University of New Hampshire, Durham, NH, Tuesday, November 1st, 2011).

2. Larry Gu and Alicia Zou, "Senior Capstone Class Visits Slaughterhouse," *Boston Latin School Argus, Page 3.*

3. "Nutrition and Healthy Eating," *Mayo Clinic*, December 3, 2011, http://www.mayoclinic.com/health/organic-food/NU00255.
4. Stephen Messenger, "College in California Becomes First to Produce More Energy Than It uses," *TreeHugger*, June 30, 2011, http://www.treehugger.com/corporate-responsibility/college-in-california-becomes-first-to-produce-more-energy-than-it-uses.html.
5. Emily Zawacki, "Lawrence among Top Twenty Schools Nation-wide for Recycling Efforts," *The Lawrentian*, last updated May 4, 2012, http://www.lawrentian.com/news/lawrence-among-top-twenty-schools-nation-wide-for-recycling-efforts-1.2866528#.T66mzOjOwvl.
6. "Renewable Energy Minor," *George Mason University College of Science*, accessed May 10, 2012, http://cos.gmu.edu/academics/undergraduate/minors/renewable-energy.
7. "Value of Soil," *Soil Quality for Environmental Health*, last updated September 19, 2011, http://soilquality.org/basics/value.html.
8. *Cornell Waste Management Institute*, accessed June 11, 2012, http://cwmi.css.cornell.edu/aboutwmi.html.
9. Philippe Menanteau, "Policy Measures to Support Solar Water Heating: Information, Incentives and Regulations," *World Energy Council*, May 2007, http://www.worldenergy.org/documents/solar_synthesis.pdf.
10. "Ocean Wave Energy," *OCS Alternative Energy and Alternate Use Programmatic EIS Information Center*, accessed June 11, 2012, http://ocsenergy.anl.gov/guide/wave/index.cfm.
11. "Newly Installed Stations to Charge up Electric Vehicles," *Cal State LA*, accessed June 11, 2012, http://www.calstatela.edu/

univ/ppa/spotlight/archive/2011/evchargingstations.php.
12. Wright, *The New York Times Almanac 2011*, 509.
13. *McGraw-Hill Dictionary of Scientific and Technical Terms*, 6th ed.
14. Lee Crockett, "Overfishing 101: A Beginner's Guide to Understanding U.S. Fishery Management," *The Pew Charitable Trusts*, March 30, 2011, http://www.pewenvironment.org/news-room/opinions/overfishing-101-a-beginners-guide-to-understanding-us-fishery-management-329418.
15. "Wind Energy: Lesson Plans and Resource Guide," *EFMR Monitoring Group*, 2009, http://www.efmr.org/edu/wind2009.pdf, 5.
16. John S. Hoffman and John Bruce Wells, "Transforming the Market for Solar Water Heaters: A New Model to Build a Permanent Sales Fohttp://.www.walkinginfo.org/training/university-courses/contacts.cfm rce," *REPP Research Report* 4 (August 1998). http://www.repp.org/repp_pubs/pdf/hoffman.pdf.
17. See National Parks Map, http://www.nps.gov/nps/customcf/apps/park-search/img/nat-map-final-1208.jpg
18. Ibid.
19. *Shelter Me; Let's Go Home*, PBS.
20. Molly Davis, "Bulldogs Study Shelter Dogs during May Term," *Redlands Daily Facts*, May 8, 2011.
21. Laurie Caplan MSC, *Causes of Cancer in Dogs*, http://www.helpyourdogfightcancer.com/CausesPrevention.shtml.
22. University of Florida College of Veterinary Medicine, Research Programs, http://research.vetmed.ufl.edu/research-programs/

Chapter Nine: A Healthier and Greener New England

1. "History of the Railroad in Danvers."
2. Ibid.
3. State of the American Dream, MassInc.
4. Timebanks, hourworld.org
5. "2010 Shape of the Nation Report: States Severely Lacking Key Physical Education Mandates That Can Help Address the Childhood Obesity Epidemic," National Coalition for Promoting Physical Activity, June 18, 2010, http://www.ncppa.org/home/news/19.
6. Safe Routes Massachusetts
7 Ethan Geiling, "Is Financial Education in the Schools in Decline?" CFED, April 4, 2012, http://cfed.org/blog/inclusiveeconomy/is_financial_education_in_schools_on_the_decline.

8. Laidler, "Free Finance Class a Hit at Salem State."
9. Strict Mass. Zoning Laws
10. Rob Eno, "Healey 50 Point Plan," Red Mass Group, March 22, 2007, http://www.redmassgroup.com/diary/141.
11. Polly Nichol, "Shared Housing Takes Many Forms," Vermont Housing & Conservation Board, accessed May 5, 2012, http://www.vhcb.org/SharedHousingArticle.html.
12. Lazar, Kate", Mass Opiod Deaths Topped 1,000 in 2014, https://www.bostonglobe.com/metro/2015/04/28/more-than-people-died-from-heroin-and-other-opioids-state-figures-show/697gYjFZS6DnuKhREzfEcO/story.html, April 28, 2015.
13. Romneycare vs. Obamacare; Similarities and Differences, CBS Local, http://boston.cbslocal.com/2013/11/13/romneycare-vs-obamacare-key-similarities-differences/
14. 2007 New York Times World Almanac
15. Northeastern School of Journalism
16. "What is Mass Health?" MassResources.org, accessed June 11, 2012, http://www.massresources.org/masshealth-description.html.
17. See Eno, "Healey 50 Point Plan," point 13: "Keep doctors in Massachusetts and reduce health care costs by adopting medical malpractice reform."
18. Masssachusetts Health Connector, https://betterhealthconnector.com/
19. Healey
20. Barbara Marquand, "Pros and Cons of Catastrophic Health Insurance," Insurance.com, March 1, 2011, http://www.insurance.com/health-insurance/coverage/pros-and-cons-of-catastrophic-health-insurance.aspx.
21. See the course description for Social Work 846: Health Policy and Services at Salem State University: http://www.salemstate.edu/academics/schools/2194.php?nbr=846&sbj=SWK&acad=GDSCH.
22. See the course description for Global Health Perspectives at BC: http://www.bc.edu/offices/international/progsummer/America/ecglobalhealth11.html
23. Federalist Comparisons
24. See the course description for Economics 308: Healthcare Economics at Wesleyan University: https://iasext.wesleyan.edu/regprod/!wesmaps_page.html?crse=003638&term=1129.
25. Goodman, Amy, The Silenced Majority,
26. Northeastern University College of Arts, Media and Design, http://www.northeastern.edu/camd/journalism/investigative-reporting/
27. Fraser, Matthew J. "Making Walker and Bike Paths Friendly," Salem News, August 21, 2014, page 11.

28. Veterans Conservation Corp., https://www.corpsnetwork.org/impact/conservation/veterans-conservation-corps, Accessed July 7, 2015
29. http://www.aspca.org/about-us/faq/pet-statistics

Chapter Ten: All Lives Matter

1. Lauren Weber and Melissa Korn, "For Most Graduates, Grueling Job Hunt Awaits," Wall Street Journal Online, May 7 2012, http://online.wsj.com/article/SB10001424052702304020104577384410323391198.html.
2. "Bicycle Lanes."
3. The basic idea expressed in point two was my own, but Matt Cardin, an author and writing instructor at McLennan Community College in Waco, Texas, developed the ideas into the clear, smooth prose that you can see above. See his online presences at www.mattcardin.com and www.teemingbrain.com.
4. Sum et al., *New Skills for the New Economy*.
5. Agresti and Cardone, "Social Security Facts."
6. This is according to Massachusetts Tax income law.
7. Glossary of Political Economy Terms, Dr. Paul Johnson, http://www.auburn.edu/~johnspm/gloss/sequestration.
8. This quote is courtesy of a story on the PBS website titled "Summary of Steve Forbes' Flat Tax Plan," *PBS Newshour*, accessed February 2, 2012, http://www.pbs.org/newshour/bb/congress/forbes_flat_tax.html.
9. Jess Halliday, "Let Food be Thy Medicine," July 11, 2005, *nutra-ingredients.com*, http://www.nutraingredients-usa.com/Industry/Let-food-be-thy-medicine.
10. Jon Huntsman, "Energy Policy" (speech, University of New Hampshire, Durham, NH, Tuesday, November 1st, 2011).
11. David Freeman, *Winning Our Energy Independence, An Energy Insider Shows How,* (Layton, Utah, Gibbs Smith, 2007).

Bibliography

"About Us." *True North*. Accessed June 7, 2012. http://www.truenorthhealthcenter.org/about.asp.

Agresti, James D. and Stephen F. Cardone. "Social Security Facts." *Just Facts*. Last modified February 20, 2012. http://www.justfacts.com/socialsecurity.asp.

Andriotis, AnnaMaria. "6 Colleges Cutting Tuition." *Yahoo! Finance*, February 10, 2012. http://finance.yahoo.com/news/6-colleges-cutting-tuition.html.

"Anxiety Statistics." *anxietycentre.com*. Accessed June 7, 2012. http://www.anxietycentre.com/anxiety-statistics-information.shtml.

Archer, Shirley. "Deep Breathing and Pain Management." *IDEA Health & Fitness Association*, November 2006. http://www.ideafit.com/fitness-library/deep-breathing-and-pain-management.

"Tai Chi Reduces Fear of Falling in Older Adults." *IDEA Health & Fitness Association*, January 2006. http://www.ideafit.com/fitness-library/tai-chi-reduces-fear-falling-older-adults.

Berman, Sheldon, Perry Davis, Ann Koufman-Frederick, and David Urion. "The Rising Costs of Special Education in Massachusetts: Causes and Effects," in *Rethinking Special Education for a New Century*, edited by Chester G. Finn, Jr., Andrew J. Rotherham, and Charles R. Hokanson, Jr., 183-211. Washington, DC: Thomas B. Fordham Foundation and Progressive Policy Institute, 2001. PDF e-book.

"Bicycle Lanes." *Walkinginfo.org*. Accessed January 26, 2012. http://www.walkinginfo.org/engineering/roadway-bicycle.cfm.

"Boston College Launches New Model for University-Wide Engagement." *The Center for Green Schools*, July 8, 2011. http://www.centerforgreenschools.org/utility-nav/blog/11-07-08/Boston_College_Launches_New_Model_for_University-Wide_Engagement.aspx.

"Brattleboro, Vermont: Changing the 'Drive to School' Culture." *Safe Routes: National Center for Safe Routes to School.* Accessed May 5, 2012. http://www.saferoutesinfo.org/data-central/success-stories/brattleboro-vermont-changing-drive-school-culture.

Brookline Tab, "Eight Awesome Benefits of Walking".

"Cancer Strategy #1: Low Oxygen Levels Breed Cancer." *Cancer Fighting Strategies.* Accessed February 20, 2012. http://www.cancerfightingstrategies.com/oxygenation.html.

Carey, Gerald T. "Social Security benefit increase no windfall." *The Salem News*, December 26, 2011. http://www.salemnews.com/opinion/x191079721/Letter-Social-Security-benefit-increase-no-windfall.

"Case Study: Arlington, Massachusetts." *Safe Routes: National Center for Safe Routes to School.* Accessed May 5, 2012. http://www.saferoutesinfo.org/program-tools/case-study-arlington-massachusetts.

Congressional Budget Office. "Federal Debt and Interest Costs." December 14, 2010. http://www.cbo.gov/publication/21960.

Cornell Waste Management Institute. Accessed June 11, 2012. http://cwmi.css.cornell.edu/aboutwmi.html.

Crockett, Lee. "Overfishing 101: A Beginner's Guide to Understanding U.S. Fishery Management." *The Pew Charitable Trusts*, March 30, 2011. http://www.pewenvironment.org/news-room/opinions/overfishing-101-a-beginners-guide-to-understanding-us-fishery-management-329418.

"Crop Mobs in Vermont." *University of Vermont Center for Sustainable Agriculture.* Last updated March 25, 2011. http://www.uvm.edu/sustainableagriculture/?Page=cropmob.html.

Dead Poets Society. Directed by Peter Weir. 1989. Burbank, CA: Walt Disney Video, 1998. DVD.

"Depression Health Center: Exercise and Depression." *WebMD.* Accessed February 4, 2012. http://www.webmd.com/depression/guide/exercise-depression.

"Depression Statistics (Adults and Teenagers) for the United States." *Cure Talk.* Accessed June 11, 2012. http://trialx.com/curetalk/2011/03/depression-statistics-adults-and-teenagers-united-state.

Dietz, Robert. "The Social Consequences of Home Ownership." Ohio State University Department of Economics and Center for Urban and Regional Analysis, 2003. Accessed February 20, 2012. http://web.mit.edu/~cwuz/Public/14.33/dietz%20social_consequences.PDF.

"Digital Media and Learning Fact Sheet." *MacArthur Foundation.* Accessed June 7. 2012. http://digitallearning.macfound.org/atf/cf/%7B7E45C7E0-A3E0-4B89-AC9C-E807E1B0AE4E%7D/DL%20FACT%20SHEET.PDF.

"Dropout Prevention." *Solutions for America.* Accessed June 7, 2012. http://www.solutionsforamerica.org/healthyfam/dropout_prevention.html.

Drum, Kevin. "Poverty and Stress." *Mother Jones,* April 5, 2009. http://motherjones.com/kevin-drum/2009/04/poverty-and-stress.

Ebbeling, Carol B., Dorota B. Pawlak, and David S. Ludwig. "Childhood Obesity: Public Health Crisis, Common Sense Cure." *Lancet* 360 (2002): 473-82. Accessed June 19, 2011. http://www.allhealth.org/briefingmaterials/lancetobesityrev-393.pdf.

"Education Facts at a Glance." *Infoplease.* Accessed June 7, 2012. http://www.infoplease.com/spot/schoolfacts1.html#ixzz1juzncCcv.

Emerson, Ralph Waldo. "The Transcendentalist" (1842 lecture). *American Transcendentalism Web.* Accessed June 11, 2012. http://transcendentalism.tamu.edu/authors/emerson/essays/transcendentalist.html.

Eno, Rob. "Healey 50 Point Plan." *Red Mass Group,* March 22, 2007, http://www.redmassgroup.com/diary/141.

Erlich, Mark. "About MassINC." Accessed June 7, 2012. http://www.massinc.org/About/Voices/Mark-Erlich2.aspx.

Fainaru-Wada, Mark. "Critical Mass Crisis: Child Obesity." *ESPN Outside the Lines,* March 26, 2009. http://sports.espn.go.com/espn/otl/news/story?id=4015831.

"Federal Budget 101: Why Should You Care about the Federal Budget?" *National Priorities Project.* Accessed June 7, 2012. http://nationalpriorities.org/budget-basics/federal-budget-101/?redirected=true#spending.

"Fitness and Exercise: Exercise for a Healthy Heart." *WebMD.* Accessed February 27, 2012. http://www.webmd.com/fitness-exercise/exercise-healthy-heart.

Geiling, Ethan. "Is Financial Education in the Schools in Decline?" *CFED*, April 4, 2012. http://cfed.org/blog/inclusiveeconomy/is_financial_education_in_schools_on_the_decline.

Geraci, Ron. "13 Ways to Naturally Boost Your Testosterone Levels." *Tim's Nutrition and Weightlifting Page*. Accessed June 11, 2012. http://www.timinvermont.com/fitness/boosttes.htm. Reprinted from *Men's Health*, December 25, 2000.

"Go Out and Play!" *The Cornell Lab of Ornithology*. Accessed June 7, 2012. http://www.birds.cornell.edu/celebration/temporary/go-outside-and-play.

Gu, Larry and Alicia Zou, "Senior Capstone Class Visits Slaughterhouse," *The Argo* Boston Latin School Newspaper, Volume XLVII, November 18, 2014.

"Health Care Statistics." *HealthCareProblems.org*. Accessed November 16, 2011. http://www.healthcareproblems.org/health-care-statistics.htm.

"Heart Failure: Exercise for a Healthy Heart." *MedicineNet.com*. Accessed February 27, 2012. http://www.medicinenet.com/fitness_exercise_for_a_healthy_heart/article.htm.

Herndon, Jaime. "What Nutrients Build Strong Tendons?" *Livestrong.com*, May 29, 2011. http://www.livestrong.com/article/306292-what-nutrients-build-strong-tendons/#ixzz1nbv09mpH.

Hinson, Sarah Lawrence. "The Power of Reflexology and How It Can Help You." *The Power of Reflexology*. Accessed June 11, 2012. http://www.reflexologypower.com.

"History of the Railroad in Danvers." *Danvers Rail Trail.* Accessed November 13, 2011. http://www.danversrailtrail.org/history.htm.

Hoffman, John S. and John Bruce Wells. "Transforming the Market for Solar Water Heaters: A New Model to Build a Permanent Sales Force." *REPP Research Report* 4 (August 1998). http://www.repp.org/repp_pubs/pdf/hoffman.pdf.

"How it Works." *Cape Ann Time bank*. Accessed December 1, 2011. http://www.capeanntimebanks.org/How_it_Works.html.

Huntsman, Jon. "Energy Policy." Speech, University of New Hampshire, Durham, NH, Tuesday, November 1st, 2011.

Killipara, Puneet. "Government still trying to catch up on foreign language capabilities." *The Hill*, June 12, 2010. http://thehill.com/homenews/senate/102833-government-still-trying-to-catch-up-on-foreign-language-capabilities.

Knight, George. "The Benefits of Treadmills for Older People." *Ezine Articles*, March 17, 2010. http://ezinearticles.com/?The-Benefits-of-Treadmills-For-Older-People&id=3950092.

LaFranchi, Howard. "US no longer towers over Latin America." *Christian Science Monitor*, April 18, 2009. http://www.csmonitor.com/USA/Foreign-Policy/2009/0418/p02s04-usfp.html.

Laidler, John. "Free Finance Class a Hit at Salem State." *Boston.com*, March 3, 2011. http://www.boston.com/news/education/higher/articles/2011/03/03/free_finance_class_a_hit_at_salem_state.

Lawson, Willow. "The Obesity-Depression Link." *Psychology Today*, May 1, 2003 (last reviewed on April 16, 2012). http://www.psychologytoday.com/articles/200305/the-obesity-depression-link.

Leighton, Paul. "High Tech Demand: Competition Fierce for Vocational School Slots." *Minuteman*, March 24, 2012. http://minuteman.org/student-life/news-happenings/in-the-news/306-high-tech-demand-competition-fierce-for-vocational-school-slots. Reprinted from *Salem News*, March 23, 2012.

Leung, Loh-Sze. "Mass. needs to expand support of 'middle-skill' jobs." *Mass High Tech*, August 18, 2010. http://www.nationalskillscoalition.org/states/state-coalitions/massachusetts/media/masshightechbusineness_2010-08-18.pdf.

Long, Bridget Terry, Dana Ansel, and Greg Leiserson. *Paying for College: The Rising Cost of Higher Education.* Boston: MassINC, 2006. http://www.massinc.org/Research/Paying-for-College.aspx.

Long, Chrissie, "Are U.S. State and Local governments on a Fiscally Sustainable Path?" Journalists Resource, *Harvard Shorenstein School on Media, Politics and Public Policy.* http://journalistsresource.org/studies/government/budget/are-u-s-state-and-local-governments-on-a-fiscally-sustainable-path.

Mahany, Brian. "IRS overwhelmed by New Tax Law Changes." *The Fraud Files.* Accessed November 29, 2011. http://www.sequenceinc.com/fraudfiles/2011/09/irs-overwhelmed-by-new-tax-law-changes.

Maine Woods National Park Project, http://www.mainewoodsnationalpark.com/the-park.html.

Marquand, Barbara. "Pros and Cons of Catastrophic Health Insurance." *Insurance.com*, March 1, 2011. http://www.insurance.com/health-insurance/coverage/pros-and-cons-of-catastrophic-health-insurance.aspx.

The Mayday Fund Special Committee on Pain and the Practice of Medicine. "A Call to Revolutionize Chronic Pain Care in America: An Opportunity in Health Care Reform." *The MayDay Fund*, 2009. http://www.maydaypainreport.org/docs/A%20Call%20to%20 Revolutionize%20Chronic%20Pain%20Care%20in%20America.pdf.

McDermott, Casey. "States Start to Require Courses in Financial Literacy." *USA Today*. Last updated August 15, 2011. http://www.usatoday.com/money/perfi/basics/2011-08-12-personal-finance-courses_n.htm.

Menanteau, Philippe. "Policy Measures to Support Solar Water Heating: Information, Incentives and Regulations." *World Energy Council*, May 2007. http://www.worldenergy.org/documents/solar_synthesis.pdf.

Messenger, Stephen. "College in California Becomes First to Produce More Energy Than It uses." *TreeHugger*, June 30, 2011. http://www.treehugger.com/corporate-responsibility/college-in-california-becomes-first-to-produce-more-energy-than-it-uses.html.

"Mortgage Default: What happens if I am a co-borrower and one of us defaults?" *PodProperty*. Accessed January 26, 2012. http://www.podproperty.com.au/faqs.php#18.

Moscovitch, Edward. *Closing the Gap; Raising Skills to Raise Wages*. Boston: Massachusetts Institute for the New Commonwealth, 1997.

"Movement and Sports Studies (Physical Education) Major." Springfield College. Accessed June 7, 2012. http://www.spfldcol.edu/homepage/dept.nsf/04E52AE2BE212E4245256BD80029D783/263541 9FC97EB65845256CF50023049F.

"Newly Installed Stations to Charge up Electric Vehicles." *Cal State LA*. Accessed June 11, 2012. http://www.calstatela.edu/univ/ppa/spotlight/archive/2011/evchargingstations.php.

Nichol, Polly. "Shared Housing Takes Many Forms." *Vermont Housing & Conservation Board*. Accessed May 5, 2012. http://www.vhcb.org/SharedHousingArticle.html.

Noble, Holcomb. B. "A Secret of Health in Old Age; Muscles." *The New York Times*, October 20, 1998. http://www.nytimes.com/1998/10/20/science/a-secret-of-health-in-old-age-muscles.html?pagewanted=all&src=pm.

"Nutrition and Healthy Eating." *Mayo Clinic*, December 3, 2011. http://www.mayoclinic.com/health/organic-food/NU00255.

"Ocean Wave Energy." *OCS Alternative Energy and Alternate Use Programmatic EIS Informatino Center*. Accessed June 11, 2012. http://ocsenergy.anl.gov/guide/wave/index.cfm.

"Osteoporosis." *The Mayo Clinic*, December 13, 2011. http://www.mayoclinic.com/health/osteoporosis/DS00128.

Quinn, Elizabeth. "Many Senior Lose Fitness Due to Lack of Training, Not Just Aging." *About.Com Sports Medicine*. Last modified May 12, 2011. http://sportsmedicine.about.com/od/olderathletes/a/seniorfit.htm.

"Paths/Trails." *MassBike*. accessed May 5, 2021. http://massbike.org/resourcesnew/pathstrails.

"Physical Health." *Time banking UK*. Accessed February 27, 2012. http://www.timebanking.org/about/timebanking-resources/research/physical-health.

Rampbell, Catherine. "How Much Americans Actually Pay in Taxes." *Economix*, *The New York Times*, April 8, 2009. http://economix.blogs.nytimes.com/2009/04/08/how-much-americans-actually-pay-in-taxes.

Reinhardt, Christianna. "Food Jobs: Arroyo Time bank." *KCET*, December 15, 2011. http://www.kcet.org/socal/food/the-nosh/food-jobs-arroyo-time-bank.html.

"Renewable Energy Minor." *George Mason University College of Science*. Accessed May 10, 2012. http://cos.gmu.edu/academics/undergraduate/minors/renewable-energy.

Repanshek, Kurt, Traveler's Five Picks for New National Parks, http://www.nationalparkstraveler.com/2013/07/travelers-five-picks-new-national-parks23553.

The Rushey Green Exchange Times, January 2011. http://www.rgtb.org.uk/Newsletters/january_11.pdf.

Scarry, Joseph T. *"Big Brother in Area Studies," The Harvard Crimson, December 5, 2003, http://www.thecrimson.com/article/2003/12/5/big-brother-in-area-studies-with/*

Schlesinger, Robert. "The Origins of That Eisenhower 'Every Gun That Is Made...' Quote." *U.S. News & World Report*, September 30, 2011. http://www.usnews.com/opinion/blogs/robert-schlesinger/2011/09/30/the-origins-of-that-eisenhower-every-gun-that-is-made-quote.

Steidle, Chris. "Low Testosterone Levels in Men." *Seek Wellness*. Last modified March 2011. http://www.seekwellness.com/andropause/low_testosterone.htm.

"Sticker Price vs. Affordability." *College Board*. Accessed December 27, 2011. http://www.collegeboard.com/student/pay/add-it-up/4494.html.

Storobin, David. "The Flat Tax Revolution in Europe." *Global Politician*, May 8, 2006. http://www.globalpolitician.com/22020-europe.

"Strength Training." *The Walking Site*. Accessed February 27, 2012. http://www.thewalkingsite.com/strength.html.

Sum, Andy, Mykhaylo Trub'skyy, Sheila Palma, John Comings, Johan Uvin, W. Neal Fogg, Maricel Santos, and Lisa Soricone. *New Skills for the New Economy*. Boston: MassINC, 2000. http://www.massinc.org/Research/New-Skills-for-a-New-Economy.aspx.

Sum, Andy, Neeta Fogg, Paul Harrington, Ishwar Khatiwada, Mykhaylo Trub'skyy, Sheila Palma, Gursel Aliyev, Jacqui Motroni, Alex Plotkin, Nathan Pond, and Abilasha Rao. *The State of the American Dream in Massachusetts, 2002*. Boston: MassINC, 2002. http://www.massinc.org/Research/The-State-of-the-American-Dream.aspx.

"Summary of Steve Forbes' Tax Plan." *PBS Newshour.* Accessed February 2, 2012. http://www.pbs.org/newshour/bb/congress/forbes_flat_tax.html.

"10 Ways You Can Help Fight Factory Farms." *ASPCA*. Accessed June 7, 2012. http://www.aspca.org/fight-animal-cruelty/farm-animal-cruelty/10-ways-you-can-help-fight.aspx.

"2010 Shape of the Nation Report: States Severely Lacking Key Physical Education Mandates That Can Help Address the Childhood Obesity Epidemic." *National Coalition for Promoting Physical Activity*, June 18, 2010. http://www.ncppa.org/home/news/19.

U.S. Census Bureau. *Bicentennial Edition; Historical Statistics of the United States, Colonial Times to 1970*. Washington, DC: 1975. http://www2.census.gov/prod2/statcomp/documents/CT1970p1-01.pdf.

U.S. Centers for Disease Control and Prevention. "Overweight and Obesity: Causes and Consequences." Last modified April 27, 2012. http://www.cdc.gov/obesity/adult/causes/index.html.

U.S. Government Printing Office. *Budget of the United States Government, Fiscal Year 2002*. Accessed June 7, 2012. http://www.gpo.gov/fdsys/browse/collection.action?collectionCode=BUDGET&browsePath=Fiscal+Year+2002&isCollapsed=false&leafLevelBrowse=false&isDocumentResults=true&ycord=0.

U.S. Office of Management and Budget. *Fiscal Year 2012 Historical Tables: Budget of the U.S. Government.* Washington, DC: Government Printing Office, 2010. http://www.whitehouse.gov/sites/default/files/omb/budget/fy2012/assets/hist.pdf.

"Value of Soil." *Soil Quality for Environmental Health.* Last updated September 19, 2011. http://soilquality.org/basics/value.html.

Watson, Stephanie. "Amazing Facts about Heart Health and Heart Disease." *WebMD.* Accessed February 27, 2012. http://www.webmd.com/heart/features/amazing-facts-about-heart-health-and-heart-disease .

Weber, Lauren and Melissa Korn, "For Most Graduates, Grueling Job Hunt Awaits," *Wall Street Journal Online,* May 7 2012, http://online.wsj.com/article/SB10001424052702304020104577384410323391198.html.

"What is Mass Health?" *MassResources.org.* Accessed June 11, 2012. http://www.massresources.org/masshealth-description.html.

"What It Costs to Go to College." *CollegeBoard.* Accessed December 27, 2011. http://www.collegeboard.com/student/pay/add-it-up/4494.html.

"Who Pays Income Taxes?" *National Taxpayers Union.* Accessed June 7, 2012. http://ntu.org/tax-basics/who-pays-income-taxes.html.

Woods, Thomas E. *Meltdown: A Free-Market Look at Why the Stock Market Collapsed, the Economy Tanked, and the Government Bailouts Will Make Things Worse.* Washington, DC: Regnery Publishing, 2009.

Wright, John C., ed.. *The New York Times Almanac 2007: The Almanac of Record.* New York: Penguin, 2006.

———, ed. *The New York Times Almanac 2011: The Almanac of Record.* New York: Penguin, 2010.

Wu, Kevin J. and Radhika Jain, Federal Funding for Harvard Declines, *The Harvard Crimson,* April 4, 2012, http://www.thecrimson.com/article/2012/4/4/centers-decrease-federal-funding/.

Zawacki, Emily. "Lawrence among Top Twenty Schools Nation-wide for Recycling Efforts." *The Lawrentian,* last updated May 4, 2012. http://www.lawrentian.com/news/lawrence-among-top-twenty-schools-nation-wide-for-recycling-efforts-1.2866528#.T66mzOjOwvl.

Zimmer, Amy. "High-Priced Neighborhoods Less Safe for Property Crime, Report Says." DNAInfo.com. Last modified September 27,2011. http://www.dnainfo.com/20110927/upper-east-side/east-west-harlem-safer-for-property-crime-than-ues-soho#ixzz1jvT8qsxU.

Index

A

B

C

D

E

F

G

H

I

J

K

L

M

N

T

U

V

W

Other Books
by
Salem House Press

Salem Secret Underground: The History of the Tunnels in the City
by Christopher Jon Luke Dowgin

A look at an attempt by early federal politicians to defraud our government within a sleepy New England town in the nineteenth century utilizing a series of tunnels..

The Ugly European
by
Dr. Peter Senn

A conversation on the European character between an advisor, the President, and a telepathic cat. Sophie's World for European History.

Anatomy of a Love Affair
by
m i keaton and Ana Steele

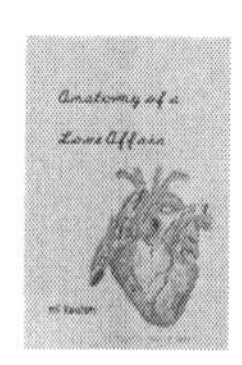

A modern love story appropriate for our screwed up times about a conversation between two organs (not those two) belonging to a mixed up couple.

Matthew J. Fraser: **is the Language Guy**

An educator specializing in Languages, he has been teaching diverse populations and listening to their concerns. An avid reader and consumer of media on what the state of the country is. Also, Matthew is a mixed martial art practitioner.